Securities and Exchange Commission: Opportunities Exist to Improve Oversight of Self-Regulatory Organizations

United States Government Accountability Office

GAO

Report to the Ranking Member,
Committee on Finance, U.S. Senate

November 2007

SECURITIES AND EXCHANGE COMMISSION

Opportunities Exist to Improve Oversight of Self-Regulatory Organizations

GAO

Accountability ★ Integrity ★ Reliability

G A O
Accountability • Integrity • Reliability

Highlights

Highlights of GAO-08-33, a report to the
Ranking Member, Committee on Finance,
U.S. Senate

SECURITIES AND EXCHANGE COMMISSION

Opportunities Exist to Improve Oversight of Self-Regulatory Organizations

Why GAO Did This Study

Self-regulatory organizations (SRO) are exchanges and associations that operate and govern the markets, and that are subject to oversight by the Securities and Exchange Commission (SEC). Among other things, SROs monitor the markets, investigate and discipline members involved in improper trading, and make referrals to SEC regarding suspicious trades by nonmembers. For industry self-regulation to function effectively, SEC must ensure that SROs are fulfilling their regulatory responsibilities. This report (1) discusses the structure of SEC's inspection program for SROs, (2) evaluates certain aspects of SEC's inspection program, and (3) describes the SRO referral process and evaluates SEC's information system for receiving SRO referrals. To address these objectives, GAO reviewed SEC inspection workpapers, analyzed SEC data on SRO referrals and related investigations, and interviewed SEC and SRO officials.

What GAO Recommends

GAO's recommendations to the SEC Chairman for enhancing SRO oversight include, among others, establishing a written framework for conducting SRO inspections, expanding the use of SRO internal review products, and enhancing information technology to improve SEC's ability to track and analyze SROs' implementation of inspection recommendations and SRO referral data. SEC agreed with the recommendations and is taking steps to address them.

To view the full product, including the scope and methodology, click on GAO-08-33.
For more information, contact Richard J. Hillman at (202) 512-8678 or hillmanr@gao.gov.

What GAO Found

To help ensure that SROs are fulfilling their regulatory responsibilities, SEC's Office of Compliance Inspections and Examinations (OCIE) conducts routine and special inspections of SRO regulatory programs. OCIE conducts routine inspections of key programs every 1 to 4 years, inspecting larger SROs more frequently, and conducts special inspections (which arise from tips or the need to follow up on prior recommendations or enforcement actions) as warranted. More specifically, OCIE's inspections of SRO surveillance, investigative, and disciplinary programs (enforcement programs) involve evaluating the parameters of surveillance systems, reviewing the adequacy of policies and procedures for handling the resulting alerts and investigations, and reviewing case files to determine whether SRO staff are complying with its policies and procedures.

GAO identified several opportunities for SEC to enhance its oversight of SROs through its inspection program. First, although examiners have developed processes for inspecting SRO enforcement programs, OCIE has not documented these processes or established written policies relating to internal controls over these processes, such as supervisory review or standards for data collection. Such documentation could strengthen OCIE's ability to provide reasonable assurances that its inspection processes and products are subject to key quality controls. Second, OCIE officials said that they focus inspections of SRO enforcement programs on areas judged to be high risk. However, this risk-assessment process does not leverage the reviews that SRO internal and external auditors performed, which could result in duplication of SRO efforts or missed opportunities to direct examination resources to other higher-risk or less-examined programs. OCIE officials told us that they plan to begin assessing SRO internal audit functions in 2008, including the quality of their work products, which would allow OCIE to assess the usefulness of these products for targeting its inspections. Finally, OCIE currently does not formally track the implementation status of SRO inspection recommendations; rather, management consults with staff to obtain such information as needed. Without formal tracking, OCIE's ability to efficiently and effectively generate and evaluate trend information, such as patterns in the types of deficiencies found or the implementation status of recommendations across SROs, or over time, may be limited.

SEC's Division of Enforcement uses an electronic system to receive referrals of potential violations from SROs. These referrals undergo multiple stages of review and may lead Enforcement to open an investigation. From fiscal years 2003 to 2006, SEC received an increasing number of advisories and referrals from SROs, many of which involved insider trading. However, SEC's referral receipt and case tracking systems do not allow Enforcement staff to electronically search all advisory and referral information, which may limit SEC's ability to monitor unusual market activity, make decisions about opening investigations, and allow management to assess case activities, among other things.

_____**United States Government Accountability Office**

Contents

Figures

Abbreviations

ALJ	administrative law judge
ARP	Automation Review Policy
CATS	Case Activity Tracking System
FINRA	Financial Industry Regulatory Authority
IG	Inspectors General
IT	information technology
MUI	matter under investigation
NYSE	New York Stock Exchange
OCC	Office of the Comptroller of the Currency
OCIE	Office of Compliance Inspections and Examinations
OIT	Office of Information Technology
OMS	Office of Market Surveillance
ORSA	Options Regulatory Surveillance Authority
SEC	Securities and Exchange Commission
SRO	self-regulatory organization
UAF	unusual activity file

United States Government Accountability Office
Washington, D.C. 20548

November 15, 2007

The Honorable Charles E. Grassley
Ranking Member
Committee on Finance
United States Senate

Dear Senator Grassley:

Self-regulatory organizations (SRO) include, among others, national securities exchanges and securities associations registered with the Securities and Exchange Commission (SEC), such as the New York Stock Exchange (NYSE) and the Financial Industry Regulatory Authority (FINRA).[1] At the time that the system of self-regulation was created, Congress, regulators, and market participants recognized that this structure possessed inherent conflicts of interest because of the dual role of SROs as both market operators and regulators. Nevertheless, Congress adopted self-regulation, as opposed to direct federal regulation of the securities markets, to prevent excessive government involvement in market operations, which could hinder competition and market innovation. Also, Congress concluded that self-regulation with federal oversight would be more efficient and less costly to taxpayers.

For industry self-regulation to function effectively, SEC must ensure that SROs are fulfilling their regulatory responsibilities. As regulators, SROs are primarily responsible for establishing the standards under which their members conduct business; monitoring the way that business is conducted; bringing disciplinary actions against their members for violating applicable federal statutes, SEC's rules, and their own rules; and referring potential

---

[1]The Securities Exchange Act of 1934 requires SROs to, among other things, be so organized and have the capacity to carry out the purposes of the act and to enforce compliance by its members and persons associated with its members with the rules and regulations of the act and the rules of the SRO. SEC approved the establishment of FINRA in July 2007. FINRA is the result of the consolidation of the former NASD (which regulated the over-the-counter market for exchange-listed and nonexchange-listed securities and provided regulatory services to markets such as the American Stock Exchange and the NASDAQ Stock Market) and the member regulation, enforcement, and arbitration operations of NYSE Regulation, Inc. (NYSE Regulation). However, NYSE Regulation, a subsidiary of NYSE, continues to be responsible for monitoring trading that occurs on NYSE and NYSE Arca, Inc., and conducting investigations of suspicious trades. Because this consolidation occurred after we finished our fieldwork, we refer to the former NASD, and not FINRA, throughout this report.

violations of nonmembers to SEC's Division of Enforcement (Enforcement). SEC oversees SROs through such actions as reviewing their rule proposals and information technology (IT) security through its Division of Market Regulation (Market Regulation), and periodically inspecting their operations through its Office of Compliance Inspections and Examinations (OCIE). OCIE inspections are intended to assess the effectiveness of SRO operations and often make recommendations intended to improve them.[2] If OCIE finds that an SRO has failed to comply with, or enforce member compliance with, SRO rules or federal securities laws, it may refer the SRO to Enforcement for further investigation and potential sanctions. More recently, recognizing the role of internal controls in promoting compliance and effectiveness within SROs, OCIE has begun focusing increased attention on the activity and work products of the internal audit function at SROs.

This report addresses your interest in the actions taken by SEC to ensure that SROs—in particular, the two largest SROs, NASD (the SRO that provided market oversight of the NASDAQ Stock Market and certain other exchanges prior to FINRA) and NYSE—are fulfilling their regulatory responsibilities by effectively monitoring and investigating suspicious trading in listed securities and, where appropriate, prosecuting misconduct involving member broker-dealers or referring potential misconduct by non-SRO members to SEC.[3] It also addresses your interest in SEC's processes for managing and acting upon referrals received by Enforcement from SROs. Specifically, this report

1. discusses the overall structure of SEC's inspection program and, more specifically, its approach to inspections of SRO surveillance, investigative, and disciplinary programs (enforcement programs);

2. evaluates certain aspects of SEC's inspection program, including guidance and planning, the use of SRO internal audit products, and the tracking of inspection recommendations; and

---

[2]SEC generally refers to its reviews of SROs, investment companies, and investment advisers as "inspections" and its reviews of registered broker-dealers as "examinations."

[3]On the basis of 2006 data, NYSE and NASD provide market oversight over the two largest exchanges in terms of domestic equity market capitalization and the value of their shares traded.

3. describes the SRO referral process to SEC's Enforcement Division and recent trends in referral numbers and related SEC investigations, and evaluates SEC's information system for advisories and referrals.

To address our first objective, we reviewed and analyzed OCIE documentation of the 11 inspections completed between March 2002 and January 2007 of NASD and NYSE enforcement programs, an OCIE memorandum to the Commission describing the SRO inspection process, and our prior work. Furthermore, we observed a demonstration of various IT systems that NASD used to monitor the markets and track investigations and disciplinary actions. We also conducted interviews with staff from OCIE, NASD, and NYSE. To address our second objective, we reviewed OCIE inspection guidance related to the review of SRO internal audit reports, guidance for bank examiners from the Board of Governors of the Federal Reserve System (Federal Reserve) and the Office of the Comptroller of the Currency (OCC), inspection guidelines developed by the Inspectors General (IG), and our prior work. In addition, we reviewed SRO internal and external audits of IT security and interviewed staff from OCIE, Market Regulation, NASD, and NYSE. Furthermore, we reviewed internal control standards for the federal government and conducted interviews with OCIE and Enforcement officials on their respective procedures for ensuring that SROs implement inspection recommendations and remedial actions required as part of enforcement actions. In addition, we reviewed and summarized the enforcement actions brought by SEC against SROs between 1995 and 2007. To address our third objective, we observed a demonstration from Enforcement staff on the division's system for receiving SRO referrals, and we interviewed Enforcement, NASD, and NYSE staff to determine how SEC manages SRO referrals and conducts investigations. To understand trends in SRO referrals and SEC investigations related to these referrals, we requested and analyzed data from SEC's referral receipt system and case tracking system from fiscal years 2003 through 2006. We inquired about checks that SEC performs on these data and determined they were reliable for our purposes.

We performed our work in Washington, D.C.; New York, New York; and Rockville, Maryland, between September 2006 and September 2007 in accordance with generally accepted government auditing standards. Appendix I provides a more detailed description of our scope and methodology.

Results in Brief

To help ensure that SROs are fulfilling their regulatory responsibilities, OCIE conducts both routine and special inspections of SRO regulatory programs. Routine inspections assess SRO enforcement, arbitration, listings, and member examination programs at regular intervals. Special inspections are conducted as warranted and encompass follow-up work on prior recommendations or enforcement actions, investigations of tips or reports, and sweep inspections.[4] OCIE's process for conducting SRO inspections includes performing background research, drafting a planning memorandum, conducting on-site reviews, holding exit interviews, and drafting a written inspection report that is reviewed and approved by the Commission. Inspection teams consist of a lead attorney and from 2 to 6 other staff reporting to an OCIE branch chief. The number of staff dedicated to SRO inspections has fluctuated in recent years, increasing from 36 to 62 between fiscal years 2002 and 2005 in response to an increase in SEC funding, but then subsequently decreasing over the following 2 years to 46 as of June 2007. OCIE officials attributed this decline to staff attrition and a recent SEC-wide hiring freeze. OCIE officials told us that inspections of SRO enforcement programs are intended to assess the design and operation of the programs to determine whether they effectively fulfill regulatory responsibilities. In these inspections, OCIE assesses the parameters of SRO surveillance systems, reviews the adequacy of SRO policies and procedures, and reviews SRO case files to determine whether SRO staff handled the resulting alerts and investigations in compliance with its policies and procedures. OCIE inspections may result in recommendations that are intended to address any deficiencies identified and improve the effectiveness of SROs.

While OCIE inspections have assessed and made recommendations to improve the effectiveness of SRO enforcement programs, we identified several opportunities for OCIE and Market Regulation to enhance their oversight of SROs by developing formal guidance, leveraging the work of SRO internal audit functions, and enhancing information systems. The following points summarize our key findings on SEC's inspection program:

- Although examiners have processes for inspecting SRO enforcement programs, OCIE has not documented these processes in an examination manual or other formal guidance. According to OCIE officials, the

[4]During a sweep inspection, OCIE probes specific activities of all SROs, or a sample of them, to identify emerging compliance issues.

uniqueness of SRO rules and surveillance systems would make it difficult to tailor a manual to all SROs and keep it current. However, other federal financial regulators that perform inspections of diverse and complex organizations have developed guidelines or standards that outline the objectives of the inspection program and functional approaches to meeting the objectives, and inspection standards developed by the IG community recommend developing and implementing written policies and procedures for internal controls over inspection processes to provide reasonable assurance over conformance with an organization's policies and procedures. Similar documentation by OCIE could help ensure uniform standards and quality controls and serve as a reference guide for new examiners.

- OCIE officials said that they focus their inspection resources on areas judged highest risk by considering factors such as when an area was last inspected, the size of the program, the results of past inspections and consultations with other SEC offices and divisions. However, OCIE's risk-assessment and inspection planning processes do not incorporate information gathered by SRO internal audit functions. Our previous work has shown that SRO internal audits covered aspects of their regulatory programs that OCIE also inspected, and could be useful for OCIE's planning purposes. In contrast, risk assessments of large banks that federal bank examiners conduct are partly based on internal audit reports, and examiners may adjust their plans to avoid duplication of effort and minimize burden to the banks. By not considering internal audit information in their risk-assessment and planning processes, OCIE examiners may be duplicating SRO efforts or missing opportunities to direct examination resources to other higher-risk or less-examined program areas.[5]

- Market Regulation could also enhance SEC oversight over SROs by further leveraging information from SRO internal audit functions regarding the security of their enforcement-related databases. These databases contain critical information about the disciplinary and other regulatory history of SRO members; SEC and other regulators rely on the accuracy and integrity of these data for conducting their own

---

[5]See GAO, *Securities Regulation: Opportunities Exist to Enhance Investor Confidence and Improve Listing Program Oversight*, GAO-04-75 (Washington, D.C.: Apr. 8, 2004). During our prior review, OCIE officials expressed concern that the routine use of SRO internal audit reports during SRO inspections would have a "chilling effect" on the flow of information between SRO internal audit staff and other SRO employees.

investigative and enforcement efforts. While Market Regulation staff conduct regular security reviews of IT systems that SEC and SROs consider important to trading operations, in accordance with SEC guidance, as well as those systems used to remit regulatory fees, these reviews are not intended to directly address the security of enforcement-related systems. NASD and NYSE internal and external auditors regularly review the security of these systems, and have generally concluded that these SROs have adequate controls in place. However, because Market Regulation does not review these reports, it has little knowledge about the comprehensiveness of SRO reviews and cannot determine whether SROs have taken the appropriate steps to secure enforcement-related information or what risks a security breach could pose.

- OCIE currently does not formally track the implementation status of inspection recommendations. Rather, according to OCIE, management consults with staff to obtain such information as needed. The number of recommendations in 11 inspection reports we reviewed ranged from 4 to 29, although OCIE officials said some inspections resulted in as many as 30 or 40 recommendations. Without formal tracking, OCIE's ability to efficiently and effectively generate and evaluate trend information—such as patterns in the types of deficiencies found or the implementation status of recommendations across SROs, or over time—as well as to develop performance measures on the effectiveness of its inspection program, may be limited. OCIE officials told us that OCIE is currently working with SEC's Office of Information Technology (OIT) to develop a new tracking system and software that will allow OCIE to generate management reports from this system in 2008.

SRO advisories—information on suspicious trading activity that does not rise to the level of a referral—and referrals, which are received electronically in Enforcement, have increased in recent years, as have related SEC investigations and enforcement actions, but the information system SEC uses to receive advisories and referrals has limitations. SROs send advisories and referrals electronically to Enforcement's Office of Market Surveillance (OMS). The advisories and referrals, which may lead to an investigation and enforcement actions, undergo multiple reviews. OMS staff apply general criteria, such as the nature of the entity and the alleged market activity, to determine whether advisories and referrals merit further review and investigation by Enforcement attorneys. Our review of SEC data found that advisories from SROs grew significantly from 5 in fiscal year 2003 to 190 in fiscal year 2006. During the same period, referrals from SROs grew from 438 to 514, or an increase of 17 percent. Numbers of SEC investigations and enforcement actions also showed a corresponding increase. We found that almost 91 percent of all advisories and almost 80 percent of SRO referrals sent to SEC during this period involved suspected insider trading activity, which Enforcement and SRO staff attribute to increased merger and acquisition activity. Although SEC received and processed an increasing number of advisories and referrals during the review period, its systems for receiving them and tracking the resulting investigations have limited capabilities for searching and analyzing information. For example, the SRO referral system only allows users to search advisories or referrals by the issuer whose stock was flagged by SRO surveillance, not by the names of individuals or hedge funds that may be associated with the suspicious trading activity. Furthermore, the referral and case tracking systems are not linked and do not allow staff to readily analyze advisory and referral trends or characteristics, such as the duration of SRO and SEC processes for receiving and responding to SRO referrals. Combined, these limitations may reduce the ability of Enforcement staff to manage the advisory and referral processes by efficiently accessing information that could help monitor unusual market activity and make decisions about opening investigations.

This report makes three recommendations designed to strengthen SEC's oversight of SROs. In summary, we recommend that the SEC Chairman (1) establish a written framework for conducting inspections of SRO enforcement programs, and broaden current guidance to SRO inspection staff to have them consider to what extent they will use SRO internal audit reports when planning SRO inspections; (2) ensure that Market Regulation makes certain that SROs include in their periodic risk assessment of their IT systems a review of the security of their enforcement-related databases, and that Market Regulation reviews the comprehensiveness and completeness of the related SRO-sponsored audits of SRO enforcement-related databases; and (3) ensure that any software developed for tracking SRO inspections includes the ability to track SRO inspection recommendations, and consider IT improvements that would increase staff's ability to search for, monitor, and analyze information on SRO advisories and referrals.

We provided a draft of this report to SEC, and the agency provided written comments that are reprinted in appendix V. In its written comments, SEC agreed with our recommendations. In response to our recommendations, SEC said that OCIE will provide its SRO inspectors with written guidance with respect to its risk-scoping techniques and compiled summary of inspection practices; will assess the quality and reliability of SRO internal audit programs and determine whether, and the extent to which, inspections can be risk-focused on the basis of SRO internal audit work; and is developing a database for, among other things, tracking the implementation status of SRO inspection recommendations. Furthermore, Market Regulation will implement our recommendation to ensure that enforcement-related databases continue to be periodically reviewed by SRO internal audit programs and that these reviews are comprehensive and complete, and Enforcement plans to consider the recommended system improvements. SEC also provided technical comments on the draft report, which were incorporated in this report as appropriate.

Background

SROs are responsible for the surveillance of the trading activity on their markets.[6] Market transactions take place on electronic or floor-based platforms. SROs employ electronic surveillance systems to monitor market participants' compliance with SRO rules and federal securities laws. Electronic surveillance systems are programmed to review trading and other data for aberrational trading patterns or scenarios within defined parameters. Also, SROs review trading as a result of complaints from the public, members, and member firms and as a result of required notifications, such as those concerning offerings. One of the key surveillance systems employed by SROs monitors the markets for insider trading. We discuss SRO surveillance systems and investigatory procedures related to insider trading in more detail in appendix II.[7]

SRO staff review alerts generated by the electronic surveillance systems to identify those that warrant further investigation. When SROs find evidence of potential violations of securities laws or SRO rules involving their members, they can conduct disciplinary hearings and impose penalties.

---

[6]As a result of a 1985 study, SEC determined that SROs had created a viable intermarket surveillance program, and terminated its then tentative Market Oversight and Surveillance System project by determining not to develop the direct surveillance capabilities the system would have allowed. See United States Securities and Exchange Commission, *Final Report to The Senate Committee on Banking, Housing, and Urban Affairs and The House Committee on Energy and Commerce: Regarding the Market Oversight and Surveillance System* (Washington, D.C.: 1985).

[7]Insider trading is the buying or selling of a security by someone who has access to material, nonpublic information about the security. It is illegal because any trading that is based on this information is unfair to investors who do not have access to the information.

These penalties can range from disciplinary letters to the imposition of monetary fines to expulsion from trading and SRO membership. SROs do not have jurisdiction over entities and individuals that are not part of their membership, and, as such, any suspected violations on the part of nonmembers are referred directly to Enforcement. SROs maintain records of their investigations and the resulting disciplinary actions as part of their internal case tracking systems. In addition, as part of their market surveillance efforts, SROs, such as NASD and NYSE, maintain databases with information on individuals and firms associated with suspicious trading activity, such as insider trading. NASD also maintains the Central Registration Depository, the securities industry online registration and licensing database. This database makes complaint and disciplinary information about registered brokers and securities firms available to the public and, in more detailed form, to SEC, other securities regulators, and law enforcement authorities.

OCIE administers SEC's nationwide examination and inspection program. Within OCIE, the Office of Market Oversight primarily focuses on issues related to securities trading activities, with the objective of evaluating whether SRO enforcement programs and procedures are adequate for providing surveillance of the markets, investigating potential violations, and disciplining violators under SRO jurisdiction. OCIE also inspects other SRO regulatory programs, which include, among others, arbitration, listings, sales practice, and financial and operational programs. As part of the latter, OCIE coordinates the compliance inspections of NASD's district offices, which are responsible for examining broker-dealer members for compliance with SRO rules and federal securities laws.

In cases where OCIE discovers potentially egregious violations of federal securities laws or SRO rules during an SRO inspection, it may refer the case to Enforcement, which is responsible for further investigating these potential violations; recommending Commission action when appropriate, either in a federal court or before an administrative law judge (ALJ); and negotiating settlements.

SEC's Market Regulation administers and executes the agency's programs relating to the structure and operation of the securities markets, which include regulation of SROs and review of their proposed rule changes. SEC has delegated authority to Market Regulation for other aspects of SRO rulemaking as well, including the authority to publish notices of proposed rule changes and to approve proposed rule changes.

OCIE Approach to SRO Inspections Focuses on Determining Whether SROs Identify Violations and Enforce and Comply with SRO Rules Effectively

OCIE conducts both routine and special inspections of SRO regulatory programs as part of its oversight efforts. We found that the SRO inspection process generally includes a planning phase, an on-site review of SRO programs, and a written report to the SRO documenting inspection findings and recommendations that is reviewed and approved by the Commission. OCIE typically staffs inspections with a lead attorney and from 2 to 6 other staff, who also work concurrently on at least 1 other SRO inspection. The number of staff dedicated to SRO inspections has fluctuated in recent years, but as of September 2007 totaled 46. According to OCIE officials, inspections of SRO enforcement programs are intended to assess the design and operation of SRO enforcement programs to determine if they effectively fulfill SRO regulatory responsibilities. As part of these inspections, OCIE takes steps to assess SRO surveillance systems, reviews SRO policies and procedures for investigating potential violations and disciplining violators of rules and laws, and reviews samples of SRO case files to determine whether SRO staff were complying with the policies and procedures.

Overall Structure of OCIE Program Encompasses Routine Inspections of Key Regulatory Programs at SROs as Well as Special Inspections

As part of its SRO oversight responsibilities, OCIE conducts both routine and special inspections of SRO regulatory programs. At regular intervals, OCIE conducts routine inspections of key regulatory programs, such as SRO enforcement, arbitration, examination, and listings programs.[8] The inspection cycles are based on the size of the SRO market and the type of regulatory program, with key programs of larger SROs, such as NYSE and NASD, being inspected from every 1 to 2 years, and smaller regional SROs from every 3 to 4 years.[9] Inspection of enforcement programs typically include a review of SRO surveillance programs for identifying potential violations of trading rules or laws, investigating those potential violations, and disciplining those who violate the rule or law. While sometimes OCIE conducts a comprehensive review of these programs, especially at the

---

[8]OCIE also lists NASD district offices as key regulatory programs with routine inspection cycles. OCIE also conducts inspections of other nonexchange SROs, which include registered clearing agencies, transfer agents, and the Municipal Securities Rulemaking Board.

[9]In addition to FINRA and NYSE, there are nine other SROs that operate or provide regulatory services to an exchange: the American Stock Exchange; the Boston Stock Exchange; the Chicago Board Options Exchange; the Chicago Stock Exchange; the International Securities Exchange; the NASDAQ Stock Market LLC; the National Stock Exchange; NYSE Arca, Inc.; and the Philadelphia Stock Exchange.

smaller SROs, often these inspections focus on a specific aspect of the programs, such as fixed income. We discuss OCIE's process for targeting their routine inspections later in this report. OCIE also conducts special inspections of SRO regulatory programs, as warranted. Special inspections typically originate from a tip or need to follow up on past inspection findings and recommendations. Special inspections also can include sweep inspections, where OCIE probes specific activities of all SROs or a sample of them to identify emerging compliance issues. According to OCIE officials, some aspect of every SRO is generally examined every year through a routine examination of a specific regulatory program or through a special inspection.

OCIE's inspection process for SROs generally includes a planning phase, an on-site review and analysis, and a final inspection report to the SRO (see fig. 1). During inspection planning, OCIE identifies the SRO program to be inspected and assigns staff who conduct initial research on the program, prepare materials for each individual inspection on the basis of the inspection's focus, and draft a planning memorandum. In preparation for the on-site inspection, OCIE typically sends an initial document request to the SRO, asking for general program information such as organizational charts and copies of SRO policies and procedures or, if OCIE is reviewing a surveillance program, logs of alerts and the resulting investigations. We discuss OCIE's review of enforcement programs in more detail later in this section. After reviewing the documents provided, staff plan the on-site phase of the inspection, which can include additional requests for specific documents, such as case files, to be made available for review while on-site. OCIE staff typically spends 1 week on-site interviewing SRO staff and reviewing SRO case files and other documentation. After the on-site visit, OCIE staff continue their analysis in the home office; conduct follow-up interviews or request additional documentation, as needed; and begin drafting the inspection report. Staff present their initial inspection findings and recommendations to the SRO in an exit interview and incorporate initial SRO responses into the draft inspection report. Once the report is drafted, staff then circulate it to other interested SEC divisions and offices—such as the Office of General Counsel, Market Regulation, or Enforcement—for their review and comment, and then submit the report to the Commission for review. Following Commission consideration and authorization, staff issue a nonpublic report to the SRO and request that the SRO respond in writing within a specified time frame, typically 30 days.[10]

Figure 1: Key Steps in OCIE's Inspection Process for SROs

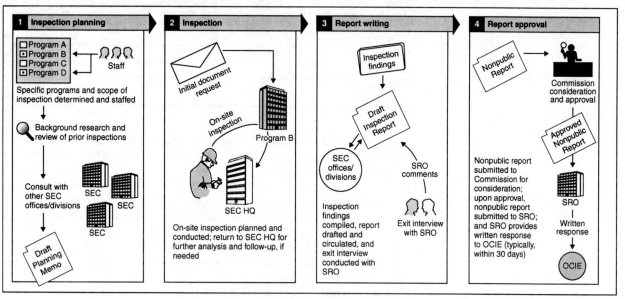

Sources: GAO (data); Art Explosion (images).

According to OCIE officials, they staff SRO inspections with a lead attorney and from 2 to 6 other staff reporting to an OCIE branch chief. These individuals are typically staffed concurrently on at least 1 other SRO inspection. As shown in table 1, as of September 2007, the SRO inspection group consisted of 46 staff, including 14 managers, 29 examiners, and 3 other support staff. Of the 32 examiners and support staff, 16 are dedicated to market oversight inspections.[11]

---

[10]Corrective actions are at times taken prior to the inspection report being issued. In this case, OCIE generally still notes the finding and recommendation in its report.

[11]Five branch chiefs and 3 assistant directors are located within the Office of Market Oversight.

Table 1: Number of OCIE Staff Delegated to SRO Inspections, Fiscal Years 2002-2007 (September)

Fiscal year	Managers			Staff		Year total
	Senior officer	Assistant director	Branch chief	Professional	Support	
2002	2	2	4	25	3	36
2003	2	2	6	27	3	40
2004	2	3	9	41	4	59
2005	2	4	9	43	4	62
2006	2	3	9	29	4	47
2007 (through Sept. 2007)	2	4	8	29	3	46

Source: OCIE.

Table 1 shows that between fiscal years 2002 and 2005, SRO inspection staffing increased from 36 to 62, or 72 percent. OCIE staff said that this increase was largely due to the increase in funding SEC received as a result of the Sarbanes-Oxley Act of 2002.[12] Since then, SRO inspection staffing has declined from 62 to 46, or 26 percent, which OCIE officials attributed to staff attrition and the inability of OCIE to hire replacements during a SEC-wide hiring freeze that occurred from May 2005 to October 2006. OCIE officials stated that despite the decrease in staff numbers, they have continued to conduct routine inspections on schedule, although the inspections may last longer than usual. Also, they said that they have not been able to do as many special inspections as they otherwise would have conducted. OCIE officials told us that the SRO inspection group recently received 6 additional professional staff positions, which it is now in the process of filling.[13]

---

[12]Congress passed the Sarbanes-Oxley Act of 2002 in response to corporate failures and fraud that resulted in substantial financial losses to institutional and individual investors. This act substantially increased SEC's appropriations. Pub. L. No. 107-204, 116 Stat. 745 (2002).

[13]OCIE officials told us that they plan to hire 6 professional staff and 1 branch chief.

GAO-08-33 Securities and Exchange Commission

OCIE Assesses Design and Operation of SRO Enforcement Programs to Determine Whether SROs Effectively Fulfill Their Regulatory Responsibilities

According to OCIE officials, inspections of SRO enforcement programs are intended to assess the design and operation of SRO enforcement programs to determine whether they effectively identify violations, enforce compliance among members, and follow their own procedures. More specifically, OCIE officials said that when inspecting SRO surveillance programs, their objectives are to determine whether (1) the parameters of SRO electronic surveillance systems are appropriately designed to generate exceptions that identify potential instances of noncompliance with SRO rules and federal securities laws and (2) the systems are effectively detecting such activity. When reviewing SRO surveillance systems, OCIE begins by asking the SRO for copies of the exchange rules that it is required to enforce, a description of the coding behind the surveillance systems designed to monitor the markets for compliance with these rules, and logs of the alerts that these systems generated. OCIE staff then review this information to determine whether the system is appropriately designed to identify noncompliance and whether it is functioning as designed. For example, as part of one inspection, OCIE staff found that the parameters of a specific surveillance system were too restrictive, after observing that the system did not generate any alerts over the inspection period. Conversely, OCIE staff said that if in reviewing a surveillance system, the inspection team saw that the system generated 10,000 alerts every quarter, they would follow up with the SRO to determine whether the indications of numerous rule violations were plausible or whether the parameters of the system were set appropriately. Either way, they said that the inspection team would dedicate resources to looking at that system.

Similarly, when evaluating SRO programs for investigating potential violations of SRO rules or federal securities laws and disciplining broker-dealer members, OCIE officials stated that their objective is to determine whether (1) SRO policies and procedures are appropriately designed to uncover violations of SRO rules and federal securities laws and to administer the appropriate disciplinary measures and (2) the SRO is complying with these policies and procedures. OCIE staff first request copies of the relevant policies and procedures for investigating surveillance alerts and for disciplining members found to be in violation of SRO rules and federal securities laws. They also ask for lists of the resulting investigations and enforcement actions, including referrals on nonmembers to SEC. OCIE staff then analyze this information to assess the extent to which SRO policies and procedures direct the SRO staff to conduct thorough reviews and investigations and, when applicable, to take appropriate disciplinary action. For example, during a recently completed sweep inspection of SRO surveillance and investigative programs related to insider trading, OCIE evaluated related SRO policies and procedures for reviewing alerts and opening investigations to determine whether they directed staff to coordinate appropriately with other SROs. We discuss the results of this sweep inspection—including a plan that the options SROs submitted to SEC to create a more uniform and coordinated method for the regulation, surveillance, investigation, and detection of insider trading—in appendix II. As part of another inspection we reviewed, OCIE found that an SRO had not yet developed formal procedures for its analysts to review alerts that were generated by a recently implemented surveillance system. OCIE recommended that the SRO develop such procedures.

When reviewing SRO enforcement programs, OCIE also assesses whether the SRO is in compliance with its own policies and procedures. To accomplish this objective, OCIE staff select and review case files pertaining to a sample of alerts, investigations, and disciplinary files from the lists that they have asked the SRO to generate. OCIE staff said when reviewing these files, they pay particular attention to the strength of the evidence upon which the SRO analyst relied in determining whether to close an alert or an investigation or to refer the case to SRO enforcement, SEC, or other appropriate regulators. In this way, OCIE staff said they can evaluate whether the SRO is enforcing its rules and federal securities laws consistently among its members and, in the case of certain federal laws such as those prohibiting insider-trading, between members and nonmembers. For example, in one inspection we reviewed, OCIE found that the SRO used its informal disciplinary measures inappropriately when disciplining its members, and recommended that formal disciplinary actions be taken when informal actions had already occurred.

OCIE inspections may result in recommendations to SROs that are intended to address any deficiencies identified and to improve SRO effectiveness. OCIE officials said that for SRO enforcement programs, they tend to make recommendations flexible enough to allow SROs to implement them in a manner that best fits their unique business models and surveillance systems. As we have previously discussed, if OCIE finds serious deficiencies at an SRO, it can refer the case to Enforcement. Such referrals are relatively infrequent—between January 1995 and September 2007, SEC brought and settled 10 enforcement actions against SROs (see app. III). According to OCIE officials, recommendation follow-up is primarily the responsibility of the examination team, under the supervision of the assistant director assigned to the inspection. Inspection follow-up begins with evaluating written responses by SROs to the inspection report and obtaining documentation of SRO efforts to address the recommendations, and can continue for several years, depending on the complexity of the recommendation. For example, OCIE officials said that some recommendations, such as those that involve the design and implementation of new information technology, may require continued dialogue with the SRO over several years before the recommendation is fully implemented. OCIE also may follow up on inspection recommendations during a subsequent inspection of the SRO. OCIE officials said that in the event the SRO does not take steps to address a recommendation that staff believe is critical, they can elevate the matter to OCIE management or the Commission, although they said that this happens infrequently. We discuss the tracking of inspection recommendations later in this report.

Written Inspection Guidance, Increased Leveraging of SRO Internal Audit Products, and IT Improvements Could Enhance SEC Oversight of SROs

We identified several opportunities for OCIE and Market Regulation to enhance their oversight of SROs by developing formal guidance, leveraging the work of SRO internal audit functions, and enhancing information systems. First, although OCIE has developed a general process for inspecting SRO enforcement programs, it has not developed an examination manual or other formal guidance for examiners to use when conducting inspections, as it has for examinations of other market participants. Such guidance could help OCIE ensure that its inspection procedures and products are subject to uniform standards and quality controls. Second, OCIE has recently expanded the use of the SRO internal and external audit reports while on-site at the SRO; however, OCIE does not leverage this work in the planning process, which could result in duplication of effort and missed opportunities to better target inspection resources. Third, in accordance with SEC policy, Market Regulation regularly inspects SRO IT systems related to market operations for adequate security controls and reviews related to SRO internal audit reports. However, this review does not target SRO enforcement-related databases, which contain investigative and disciplinary information that SROs maintain and upon which other regulators rely. Finally, OCIE currently does not formally track the implementation status of inspection recommendations, which ranged as high as 29 in the inspections that we reviewed. The lack of formal tracking may reduce OCIE's ability to efficiently and effectively generate and evaluate trend information, such as patterns in the types of deficiencies found or the implementation status of recommendations across SROs, or over time.

Lack of Formal Guidance for Inspections of SRO Enforcement Programs Could Limit OCIE's Ability to Ensure Staff Compliance with Internal Controls

Our interviews with OCIE officials and reviews of selected inspection workpapers indicated that OCIE examiners typically follow a general process when conducting reviews of SRO enforcement programs. This process begins with examination planning, is followed by data gathering, and ends with reporting. However, OCIE has not developed an examination manual or other formal guidance for its examiners to use when conducting inspections of SRO enforcement programs. According to OCIE officials, because SRO rules and corresponding surveillance systems are unique and constantly evolving, it would be difficult to develop a detailed inspection manual that could be tailored to all SROs and also remain current. These officials said that an examination manual is not necessary to ensure consistency among SRO inspections because the SRO inspection group is a relatively small group within OCIE, and all of the staff are centralized in headquarters. On the other hand, they said that because OCIE's inspection program for investment companies, investment advisers, and broker-dealers has hundreds of examiners across SEC headquarters and its regional offices who are responsible for examining thousands of firms, OCIE has developed detailed inspection manuals to ensure consistency across examinations of these firms. Similarly, OCIE officials said that they have developed guidelines for SRO examiners conducting oversight inspections of NASD's district offices because OCIE relies on examination staff in the SEC regional offices to assist them in conducting these inspections.

In contrast to OCIE, federal banking regulators, such as the Federal Reserve and OCC, have developed written guidance for the examination of large banks—also highly complex and diverse institutions—that outlines the objectives of the program and describes the processes and functional approaches used to meet those objectives. By not establishing written guidance for conducting inspections of SRO enforcement and other regulatory programs, OCIE may be limiting its ability to ensure that its inspection processes and products are subject to basic quality controls in such areas as examination planning, data collection, and report review. For example, in several of the inspections we reviewed, we did not find evidence of supervisory review, which is a key aspect of inspection quality control. According to OCIE officials, the team leader is expected to review the work of team members. However, without written policies and procedures specifying how and when this review is to be conducted and documented, it is difficult to establish whether the team leaders comply with this quality control. According to inspection standards developed by the IG community, each organization that conducts inspections should develop and implement written policies and procedures for internal controls over its inspection processes to provide reasonable assurance over conformance with organizational policies and procedures. As another example, when conducting inspections of SRO enforcement programs, OCIE officials said that team leaders often require their teams to use data collection instruments, such as checklists, when reviewing SRO files to ensure a consistent and complete review of all of the files selected, particularly when there are inexperienced staff on the team. While potentially an effective means of collecting data, according to OCIE officials, the decision to use these tools is up to the individual team leader, and not all teams employ them. According to IG inspection standards, evidence developed under an effective system of internal controls generally is more reliable than evidence obtained where such controls are lacking. By not establishing standards addressing quality controls in data collection, OCIE's ability to ensure the consistency and reliability of data collected across its SRO inspection teams may be limited. Furthermore, without written guidelines, new examiners lack a reference tool that could facilitate their orientation in the inspection program.

OCIE's Limited Use of SRO Internal Audit Reports in Inspection Planning May Diminish Opportunities to Better Target Inspection Resources

While OCIE employs a risk-based approach to conducting SRO inspections, OCIE's risk-assessment and inspection planning processes do not incorporate information gathered through SRO internal audits. According to OCIE officials, OCIE tailors inspections of SRO programs (particularly at the two largest SROs) to focus on those areas judged to pose the greatest risk to the SRO or the general market. In determining which areas present the highest risk, OCIE officials said they consider such factors as the amount of time that has passed since a particular area was last inspected, the size of the area, the results of past inspections, and consultations with other SEC offices and divisions. For example, because the enforcement programs at NASD and NYSE encompass hundreds of surveillance systems, OCIE officials said examiners cannot review all systems as part of one inspection. As a result, OCIE officials said examiners first conduct a preliminary analysis of requested documents and focus inspection resources on those systems or areas that are judged to pose the greatest risk. According to OCIE officials, because the regional SROs have smaller programs, OCIE staff typically are able to conduct a more comprehensive review of the entire enforcement program during a single inspection.

We previously recommended that OCIE develop and implement a policy requiring examiners to routinely use SRO internal review reports in planning and conducting SRO inspections.[14] Prior to October 2006, OCIE's practice was to request SRO internal audit reports only when OCIE believed specific problems existed at an SRO. In October 2006, OCIE issued a memorandum broadening the circumstances in which OCIE would request and use these reports. The memorandum directs examiners to request that SROs make all internal audit reports related to the program area under inspection available for the staff's on-site review, including workpapers or any reviews conducted by any regulatory quality review unit of the SRO or an outside auditor. According to the memorandum, on-site review of these reports may be useful in determining whether the SRO has identified particular areas of concern in a program area and adequately addressed those problems, assessing whether an SRO addressed prior inspection findings and recommendations, and helping staff determine whether they should limit or expand their review of particular issues during an inspection.

OCIE staff said that in fiscal year 2008, they also plan to begin reviewing the internal audit functions of SROs, with the goal of determining whether SRO internal audit functions are effective. For example, OCIE officials said that they plan to evaluate whether the internal audit functions are independent of SRO management, conduct thorough reviews of all relevant areas (particularly, regulatory programs), and have sufficient staffing levels. OCIE officials said that as part of their reviews, they also plan to assess the quality and reliability of SRO internal audit reports and assess whether SROs have implemented the recommendations resulting from these reports. OCIE officials told us that they are in the planning phase of this review, and, as such, they have not yet developed written guidance for their examiners in conducting these reviews.[15]

---

[14]GAO-04-75.

[15]A requirement for registration as a national securities exchange or national securities association is that the SRO have the capacity to enforce compliance of it members with SRO rules and with the federal securities laws and rules. However, OCIE officials stated that there is no SEC rule that expressly requires SROs to have an internal audit program with prescribed characteristics.

While OCIE's October 2006 memorandum broadened the use of SRO internal audit reports to encompass on-site reviews during inspections, it did not address the use of internal audit reports for planning purposes, as we had recommended. In contrast, the risk assessments of large banks that federal bank examiners conduct during the planning phase are based, in part, on internal audit reports, and examiners may adjust their examination plans to avoid duplication of effort and minimize burden to the bank. For example, according to examination guidance that the Federal Reserve issued, to avoid duplication of effort and burden to the institution, examiners may consider using these workpapers and conclusions to the extent that examiners test the work performed by the internal or external auditors and determine it is reliable. Similarly, examination guidance issued by OCC states that examiners' assessments of a bank's audit and control functions help leverage OCC resources, establish the scope of current and future supervisory activities, and assess the quality of risk management.

By not considering the work and work products of SRO internal audit functions in its inspection planning process, OCIE examiners may be duplicating SRO efforts, causing regulatory burden, or missing opportunities to direct examination resources to other higher-risk or less-examined program areas. For example, our previous work, which focused on the listing programs of SROs, showed that SRO internal audit functions had examined or were in the process of examining aspects of their listing programs that OCIE had covered in its most recent inspections, and that resulting reports could be useful to OCIE in planning as well as conducting inspections.[16] As OCIE begins to assess the quality of SRO internal audit functions and work products, the opportunity exists for OCIE to further leverage these products in targeting its own inspection efforts. OCIE

---

[16]SEC has recognized that a strong internal audit function contributes to how effectively SROs fulfill their regulatory responsibilities. On at least two occasions, SEC recommended that SROs strengthen this function to improve their oversight. First, an investigation that SEC began in 1994 into the operations and investigations of NASD and the market-making activities of NASDAQ found that NASD failed over a period to conduct an appropriate inquiry into the anticompetitive actions among NASDAQ market markers. In responding to SEC's resulting recommendations, NASD agreed to ensure the existence of a "substantial" independent review staff reporting directly to NASDAQ's Board of Governors. Second, SEC reported in 1999 that its investigations of the activity of NYSE floor brokers found that NYSE failed to dedicate sufficient resources to allow regulatory staff to perform certain required examinations of floor-broker activity. To address SEC's resulting recommendation, NYSE agreed to maintain its Regulatory Quality Review Department as a "substantial" independent internal review staff with adequate resources to regularly review all aspects of NYSE. (See app. III for additional information on these investigations.)

officials said that as part of their upcoming reviews of SRO internal audit functions, they will assess whether SRO internal audit products may be helpful in assisting them in targeting inspections of particular SRO functions.

OCIE could also further leverage the work performed by SRO internal and external auditors to monitor a particular regulatory program between inspections. In our review of OCIE inspections of NASD and NYSE enforcement programs, as many as 8 years passed between inspections of a particular surveillance system and related investigations and disciplinary actions. Moreover, as OCIE officials noted, the recent decline in SRO inspection staff has lengthened the time it takes to complete a routine SRO inspection and limited their ability to conduct additional special inspections. Unless OCIE regularly informed itself of the results of SRO efforts to review these systems, it may not know of emerging or resurgent issues until the next inspection.[17]

SEC Does Not Obtain Information on the Security of SRO Enforcement-Related Systems and Databases

As we have previously discussed, SROs conduct surveillance of trading activity on their markets; carry out investigations; and bring disciplinary proceedings involving their own members or, when appropriate, make referrals to SEC when the suspicious activity involves nonmembers. However, SEC's Market Regulation does not obtain information on the security of SRO enforcement-related databases—IT applications for storing data about SRO investigations and disciplinary actions taken against SRO members—when conducting reviews of IT security at SROs. Under SEC's Automation Review Policy (ARP), Market Regulation conducts on-site reviews of SRO trading systems, information dissemination systems, clearance and settlement systems, and electronic communications networks and makes recommendations for improvements when

---

[17]SEC enforcement actions and inspections over the past several years have highlighted weaknesses in the effectiveness of certain regulatory programs and raised questions whether, in certain circumstances, SROs have maintained regulatory programs that are sufficiently rigorous to detect, deter, and discipline for member' violations of the federal securities laws and rules and SRO rules. Accordingly, SEC is currently considering the adoption of new rules and the amendment of existing rules designed to provide greater transparency to, among other things, key aspects of the regulatory operations of national securities exchanges and registered securities associations. OCIE officials believe these rules would allow OCIE to better monitor SRO activities between inspections. See *Fair Administration and Governance of Self-Regulatory Organizations, et al.*, 69 Fed. Reg. 71126 (Dec. 8, 2004) (proposed rule).

GAO-08-33 Securities and Exchange Commission

necessary.[18] Market Regulation also conducts reviews of SRO general and application controls over the collection of fees under section 31 of the Securities Exchange Act of 1934.[19] These are IT systems designated for remitting fees to SEC as part of the section 31 program, which ensures that the data produced by these systems are authorized, and completely and accurately processed and reported.

Market Regulation officials said that they do not target enforcement-related databases for specific review, since the ARP policy statement is specifically intended to oversee systems essential to market operations. These officials said that Market Regulation could include a review of the security of enforcement-related databases both in their general assessments of SRO IT infrastructure security within the ARP and in section 31 reviews. They explained that both of these reviews include testing of components and evaluations of general access controls and changes made within SRO organizationwide network structures in their routine reviews of specific IT programs and systems, such as SRO computer operations, security assessments, internal and external audit IT coverage, and systems outage notification procedures and systems change notifications. However, these general assessments by Market Regulation would not necessarily provide SEC with information on potential risks specific to the security of the data contained in enforcement-related databases.

NASD and NYSE officials told us that they conduct their own regular internal inspections of security of IT systems, which include reviews of enforcement-related databases. In addition, both SROs contract with external companies that regularly conduct reviews of the security controls

---

[18]SEC's Policy Statement regarding Automated Systems of Self-Regulatory Organization issued in 1989 set for SEC's expectation that SROs establish comprehensive planning and assessment programs to determine the capacity and vulnerability of their IT trading and market information systems. The statement also provides guidance on the components of such a program, which included independent reviews and notification processes for system changes and outages. See *Automated Systems of Self-Regulatory Organizations, Exchange Act Release No. 27445* (Nov. 16, 1989), published in 54 Fed. Reg. 48703 (Nov. 24, 1989). Under the ARP, SEC staff conduct reviews of how SROs are addressing SEC's expectations in these areas. For further information on ARP, see GAO, *Financial Market Preparedness: Significant Progress Has Been Made, but Pandemic Planning and Other Challenges Remain*, GAO-07-531 (Washington, D.C.: Mar. 29, 2007).

[19]Section 31 of the Securities and Exchange Act requires SEC to collect transaction fees designed to cover the cost to the government of the supervision and regulation of the securities markets, including costs associated with administrative, enforcement, and rulemaking activities. 15 U.S.C. § 78ee.

of their technology systems. We reviewed several of these internal and external audits, which include reviews of SRO enforcement-related systems and databases conducted from fiscal years 2002 through 2006. These reviews generally concluded that NASD and NYSE have adequate controls in place to protect sensitive enforcement-related data.

The internal and external audit reports of NYSE and NASD that we reviewed showed that these reports could be a valuable source of information for Market Regulation on specific risks to enforcement-related databases. Market Regulation officials said that in conducting ARP-related inspections, they review SRO internal and external audit reports related to the infrastructure of SRO IT systems; however, they do not specifically look for information related to the assessment of security of enforcement-related databases. In addition, SEC staff said that although they generally receive all the internal and external audit reports done of SRO systems relating to trading and clearing functions, they may not always receive such reports relating to other systems, including enforcement-related databases, from all SROs.

Since SROs, SEC, and other regulators rely on the accuracy and integrity of the data in SRO enforcement-related databases in fulfilling their own regulatory responsibilities, protecting this information from unauthorized access is critical to regulatory efforts. For example, as we discuss later in this report, SEC uses SRO surveillance data in carrying out its own enforcement efforts related to securities trading. Furthermore, SROs are responsible for maintaining complaint and disciplinary data on their members—information that is essential for identifying recidivists. By not periodically obtaining information to ensure that the SRO risk-assessment process and SRO-sponsored audits continue to be included in SRO assessment cycles and that the audits are comprehensive and complete, Market Regulation cannot assess whether SROs have taken the appropriate steps to ensure the security of sensitive enforcement-related information, or the level of risk that a data breach could pose.

Lack of Formal Tracking System May Limit OCIE's Ability to Effectively Assess SRO Implementation of Inspection Recommendations

Although OCIE officials said that they have worked with SROs to address the intent of recent inspection recommendations, we were not able to readily verify the status of the recommendations in the inspections we reviewed because OCIE does not formally track inspection recommendations or the status of their implementation. OCIE officials said that when OCIE management is interested in obtaining an update on the recommendations resulting from an inspection, they consult directly with the examination team assigned to the SRO inspection. OCIE officials also said that they do not consider the lack of a formal tracking system to have affected their ability to manage any follow-up of inspection recommendations because there are relatively few SROs, and OCIE staff is in frequent contact with them. OCIE's informal methods for tracking inspection recommendations contrast with the expectations set by federal internal control standards for ensuring that management has relevant, reliable, and timely information regarding key agency activities.[20] These standards state that key information on agency operations should be recorded and communicated to management and others within the entity and within a time frame that enables management to carry out its internal control and other responsibilities.

Without a formal tracking system, the ability of OCIE management to effectively and efficiently monitor the implementation of SRO inspection recommendations and conduct programwide analyses may be limited. Of the 11 inspections of NASD and NYSE enforcement programs we reviewed, the number of recommendations OCIE made ranged from 4 to 29, with an average of 11.[21] They also ranged in complexity, from asking the SRO to update its policies and procedures to recommending that an SRO implement an entire surveillance program. For example, we observed recommendations calling for, among other things, improving case file documentation, changing the parameters of a surveillance system, implementing an automated tracking system, and improving SRO member education. OCIE officials said that some inspections resulted in as many as 30 or 40 recommendations. Without a formal tracking system, OCIE management must rely on staff's availability and ability to recall recommendation-related information, which may be reliable when discussing an individual inspection, but may limit OCIE management's ability to efficiently generate and evaluate trend information, such as patterns in the types of deficiencies found or the implementation status of recommendations across SROs, or over time. Implementing a formal tracking system would not only allow management to more robustly assess the recommendations to SROs and their progress in implementing them, but would allow it to develop performance measures that could assist management in evaluating the effectiveness of its inspection program.

---

[20]GAO, *Standards for Internal Control in the Federal Government*, GAO/AIMD-00.21.3.1 (Washington, D.C.: November 1999).

[21]Between fiscal years 2002 and 2006, OCIE completed an average of 42 inspections of SROs per year.

According to OCIE and SEC's OIT officials, OCIE recently began working with OIT to develop a new examination tracking system that will include the capability to track SRO responses and implementation status of OCIE recommendations. OCIE officials said that planned requirements for the system includes a field to enter the recommendation, a field for OCIE inspectors to broadly categorize the status of its implementation, and a text box for inspectors to elaborate on the recommendation and its implementation status. OCIE officials also said that they expect that the system will be able to trace the history of a recommendation. OIT officials told us that they are developing separate software that will allow OCIE to generate management reports using data from the tracking systems as well as other database; however, the requirements for any management reports OCIE would receive have yet to be determined. According to an OCIE official, the recommendation tracking system and reporting capabilities may be an effective way to provide OCIE management with a high-level characterization of implementation status. OCIE officials said that in response to our concerns, they plan to deploy an interim, stand-alone recommendation tracking system that will provide a management report, in the form of a spreadsheet, that contains all open recommendations to SROs resulting from SRO inspections and the current status of SRO efforts to implement them. These officials said that they expect to use this spreadsheet until the previously described OIT projects are implemented in 2008.

SRO Advisories and Referrals Have Increased, as Have Related SEC Investigations and Enforcement Actions, but Information Systems for Advisories and Referrals Have Limitations

Enforcement receives advisories and referrals, which undergo multiple stages of review and may lead to opening an investigation, through an electronic system in OMS. After opening investigations, Enforcement further reviews the evidence gathered to decide whether to pursue civil or administrative actions, or both. From fiscal years 2003 to 2006, OMS received an increasing number of advisories and referrals from SROs, such as NYSE and NASD, most of which involved insider trading. However, limited search capabilities of the SRO system and the lack of a link between the SRO and case activity tracking systems have limited Enforcement staff's ability to electronically search advisory and referral information, monitor unusual market activity, make decisions about opening matters under inquiry (MUI) and investigations, and assess case activities.

OMS Uses a Multistep Process to Review SRO Referral Information That Can Lead to Opening Investigations and Subsequent Enforcement Actions

Upon receipt of SRO information in its Web-based SRO Referral Receipt System (SRO system), OMS makes initial decisions on referrals and forwards selected referral materials to investigative attorneys. After initial reviews by OMS staff, Enforcement may decide to open investigations if it determines evidence garnered during its inquiry period warrants doing so and staff and financial resources are available. If investigation evidence merits, staff may pursue administrative or civil actions and seek remedies, such as cease-and-desist orders and civil monetary penalties.

Enforcement Receives Advisories and Referrals from SROs about Unusual Market Activity through a Web-Based System

The referral process begins when OMS staff receive SRO advisories and referrals on unusual market activity through a secure Web-based electronic system called the SRO system. SEC officials noted that SRO referrals help SEC identify and respond to unusual market activity by those who are not members of SROs, investigate those suspected of potentially illegal behavior, and take action when the circumstances of cases and evidence are appropriate. OMS branch chiefs, who are responsible for reviewing advisories and referrals, access the SRO system on a weekly basis to review all SRO-submitted advisories and referrals.

SRO advisories and referrals usually consist of a short form with basic background information on the suspected unusual market activity by SRO nonmembers that includes the name of the security issuer, date of the unusual activity, and a description of the market activity identified by the SRO. The materials also contain a text attachment, which includes more detailed narrative information, such as a chronology of unusual activity and specific information about issuers and individuals potentially associated with that activity. SEC does not receive information electronically or otherwise on unusual market activity by SRO members or related investigations by SROs of the unusual member activity.

OMS Reviews Both Advisories and Referrals, and Forwards Referrals to Enforcement Attorneys for Possible Investigatory Action

After reading advisories and referrals, OMS branch chiefs use SEC's National Relationship Search Index, an electronic system that connects to and works with a range of other SEC systems, such as the Case Activity Tracking System (CATS), to determine whether existing SEC investigations involve the issuer noted in the SRO advisory or referral.[22] If an investigation already exists that involves the issuer noted in the advisory or referral, the

---

[22]SEC uses CATS to record key information about MUIs, investigations, actions, and case outcomes. This information includes basic background on cases SEC has opened, dates for case milestones, and eventual case outcomes.

branch chiefs will forward the advisory or referral to the Enforcement attorney conducting that investigation for review and incorporation into his or her case.

If Enforcement has not already opened an investigation on a particular issuer, OMS staff store advisories in the SRO system, but do not investigate them because they do not contain information as detailed as that found in referrals in the SRO system.[23] However, SROs may continue their market surveillance efforts on an advisory, further develop information on the unusual market activity, and submit all information later as a referral for potential action by SEC. For referrals, branch chiefs apply criteria—such as (1) the nature of the unusual market activity, (2) the persons involved and their employment positions, (3) the dollar value of the unusual activity in question, (4) potential harm to the financial markets and individual investors, and (5) any other information branch chiefs may have obtained through conversations with SRO staff—to make initial decisions about the merit of forwarding the referrals to Enforcement management and attorneys for possible SEC investigation. Enforcement associate directors review and either approve or disapprove branch chiefs' recommendations about the referrals. Referrals not recommended by branch chiefs for approval are stored in the SRO system and may be accessed as needed.

If approved, OMS branch chiefs open an MUI, a 60-day initial inquiry period, and electronically forward all referral information to SEC headquarters or the appropriate regional office, where investigative attorneys and management have up to 60 days to review all available case information and consider staff and financial resources to decide whether to proceed with a full investigation. Once the MUI has been opened, Enforcement staff assigns the MUI a CATS case number, and staff use CATS to track all components of the case until it is closed.[24] Figure 2 outlines

---

[23]Enforcement officials said that although advisories generally do not contain enough information to warrant opening an MUI, they found this sharing of information useful in staying abreast of and potentially responding to unusual market activity.

[24]Referrals that do not become MUIs are closed, but information on the referrals still resides in the SRO system. If MUIs approved by OMS branch chiefs and Enforcement associate directors involve issuers or individuals in multiple states or in Washington, D.C., MUIs may be assigned to headquarters Enforcement staff for review and decisions on whether to fully investigate. Otherwise, branch chiefs assign MUIs to the appropriate SEC regional office. For example, an MUI that contains information about suspected insider trading activity among individuals in a New York firm would be referred to SEC's New York Regional Office.

SEC's process and average time frames for receiving, processing, and investigating unusual market activity identified by SROs.

Figure 2: SEC's Process and Average Time Frames for Receiving SRO Advisories and Referrals and Conducting Related Investigations

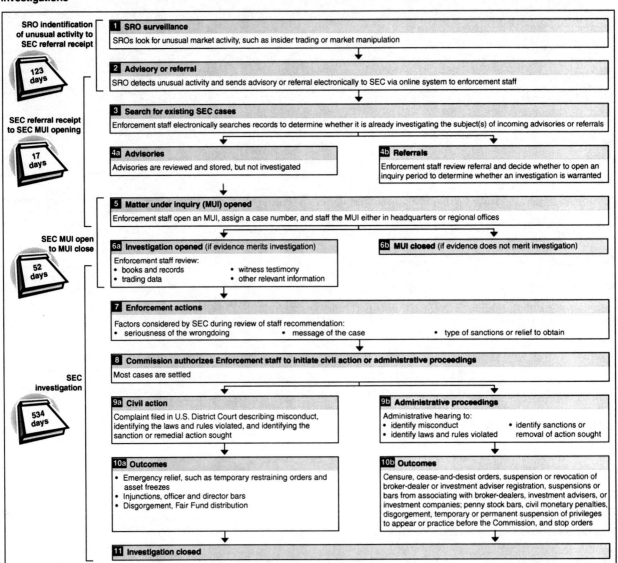

Source: GAO.

GAO-08-33 Securities and Exchange Commission

Enforcement staff at headquarters or the regional offices use criteria that are similar to those used by OMS staff during their initial review, but also consider the level of financial resources available for investigations and the availability of Enforcement staff to determine whether to close the MUI or open an investigation. If Enforcement staff do not open an investigation, the MUI is closed in CATS and staff document the reason(s) for closure, which may include insufficient evidence, resource limitations, or a newly opened case being merged with an existing case.

When Evidence from Investigation Merits, Enforcement Division Can Pursue Civil and Administrative Actions

If the Enforcement Division develops evidence it deems sufficient for moving forward, SEC may institute civil or administrative enforcement actions, or both. When determining how to proceed, Enforcement staff consider such factors as the seriousness of the wrongdoing, the technical nature of the matter under investigation, and the type of sanction or relief sought. When the misconduct warrants it, SEC will bring both types of proceedings. With civil actions, SEC files a complaint with a federal district court that describes the misconduct, identifies the laws and rules violated, and identifies the sanction or remedial action that is sought. For example, SEC often seeks civil monetary penalties and the return of illegal profits, known as disgorgement. The courts also may bar or suspend an individual from serving as a corporate officer or director (see fig. 2).

SEC can seek a variety of sanctions through administrative enforcement proceedings as well. An ALJ, who is independent of SEC, presides over a hearing and considers the evidence presented by the Enforcement staff as well as any evidence submitted by the subject of the proceeding. Following the hearing, the ALJ issues an initial decision, which contains a recommended sanction. Administrative sanctions or outcomes include cease-and-desist orders, suspension or revocation of broker-dealer and investment adviser registration, censures, bars from association with certain persons or entities in the securities industry, payment of civil monetary penalties, and return of illegal profits. Both Enforcement staff and the defendant may appeal all or any portion of the initial decision to SEC Commissioners, who may affirm the decision of the ALJ, reverse the decision, or remand it for additional hearings. An SRO may also agree to undertake other remedial actions in a settlement agreement with SEC.

Once civil or administrative proceedings have concluded and all outcomes are finalized, SEC closes the investigation and terminates the case in CATS.[25]

Figure 2 also provides data on the durations involved with referral and investigation processes and shows that stages of the process—from SRO identification of unusual market activity to the closure of investigations— vary in their duration. We analyzed data SEC provided from its referral and case tracking systems from fiscal years 2003 to 2006. For those cases for which the data had open and close dates for the investigation stage of the process, it took an average of 726 days or almost 2 years from the point that SROs identify unusual market activity and send SEC referrals to the time that SEC completely investigates and concludes cases.[26] Of this total time, it took, on average, 192 days for the first three steps in the process, which include SROs identifying unusual market activity and referring it to SEC and SEC opening an MUI to conduct its initial inquiry on referrals.[27] It took, on average, another 534 days for SEC to investigate that unusual market

---

[25]According to SEC Enforcement officials, SEC's case tracking system records the beginning of an investigation when Enforcement staff decide to investigate MUIs and open an investigation. The investigation is officially closed in the system after administrative or district court proceedings have concluded and all outcomes, such as fines, other penalties, and disgorgement, have been collected and distributed. The investigation average calculated in footnote 23 therefore includes cases that are filed or instituted as litigated matters, which require additional time for interim steps, such as discovery depositions and trial. The average also includes matters where a party is given an extended time in which to pay disgorgement or penalties, due to his or her financial condition. It also includes matters where additional noninvestigative time is spent distributing funds to investors through a disgorgement or Fair Fund. The investigation is not formally closed in CATS until all such additional steps are completed.

[26]The overall referral and investigation processes duration of 726 days, or almost 2 years, consists of a 123-day average for issue identification and SEC referral receipt, 17-day average for SEC to open an MUI, 52-day average for SEC to determine whether to investigate a matter, and 534-day average for SEC to open an investigation and completely conclude a case (see fig. 2).

[27]We calculated the 123-day average duration between SRO issue identification and SEC referral receipt using data from the SRO system on formal referrals. The 123-day average does not include earlier contact by SROs, which may make telephone referrals that may predate formal referrals. In addition, we calculated the 17-day average duration between SEC referral receipt and SEC MUI opening using data on MUIs that SEC opened after receiving referrals from SROs. The 17-day average does not include instances when SEC opened an MUI before receiving an SRO referral.

activity; institute administrative or civil enforcement proceedings; administer outcomes, such as issuing and collecting fines; and completely close investigations.[28]

From Fiscal Years 2003 through 2006, the Number of SRO Advisories and Referrals and SEC Investigations and Enforcement Actions Significantly Increased

Data we reviewed from SEC's SRO system and CATS showed that the number of advisories, referrals, and investigations significantly increased from fiscal years 2003 through 2006. More specifically, advisories increased from 5 in fiscal year 2003 to 190 in fiscal year 2006 and totaled 390 for the period. Of the 4-year total, 354, or 91 percent, were insider trading advisories, and an additional 3 percent involved market manipulation issues. Data from SEC's SRO system on 1,640 referrals showed that the number of referrals SEC received from SROs grew from 438 in fiscal year 2003 to 514 in fiscal year 2006, an increase of 17 percent. Of the total number of referrals, almost 80 percent involved suspected insider trading activities. In addition, NYSE and NASD submitted 1,095, or almost 70 percent, of the total number of referrals. SEC and SRO officials attributed the increase to more merger and acquisition activity in the marketplace.

Data SEC provided to us from its case tracking system showed a corresponding increase in the number of investigations SEC opened from SRO referrals over the same period. The number of investigations rose from 82 in fiscal year 2003 to 208 in fiscal year 2006, an increase of 154 percent. Case actions, which follow SEC's determination of whether to file a case as an administrative proceeding or a civil action, also increased. The number of case actions rose from 2 in fiscal year 2003 to 29 in fiscal year 2006. SEC actions result in case outcomes such as permanent injunctions, preliminary injunctions, restraining orders, administrative proceeding orders, and emergency actions. These case outcomes rose from 3 in fiscal year 2003 to 82 in fiscal year 2006. Case outcomes also may include "relief," such as disgorgement, payment of prejudgment interest and other monetary penalties, asset freezes, and officer and director bans.

---

[28]We calculated average investigation duration by using 189 of 574 total investigations opened during the period of our review that had open and close dates, and therefore could be used to calculate the average duration. Of the 574 investigations SEC opened during our review period, the remaining 385 (or two thirds) were ongoing or active as of the date SEC provided us with these data (Apr. 18, 2007) and were not used to calculate the 534-day average duration for investigations. We determined that as of this date, these active cases had been open an average of 696 days. Appendix IV provides additional information on these cases.

For example, in 2003, NYSE referred unusual market activity to SEC after suspecting potential insider trading activity. After opening an MUI and investigating the activity, the case resulted in an administrative proceeding and a civil action. The case resulted in a range of outcomes against 6 individuals. The administrative proceeding specifically resulted in an order barring individuals alleged in the case from associating with one another on trading. The civil action resulted in permanent injunctions to stop the suspected use of material, nonpublic information and in financial penalties that included disgorgement.

Figure 3 illustrates the upward trend in the numbers of advisories, referrals, MUIs, investigations, case actions, and case outcomes for the period we reviewed.[29] The figure also shows that more than three quarters of the referrals were made for insider trading. Market manipulation and "other" activity, including activity associated with issuer reporting and financial disclosure and initial securities offerings, constituted the other major categories of referrals. Appendix IV provides additional data on these trends by fiscal year.

---

[29]Figure 3 is not drawn to scale. Data found in this figure have two sources. The SRO system is the source of data on the number of advisories and referrals, while CATS is the source for the data on MUIs, investigations, actions, and case outcomes.

Figure 3: SRO Advisories and Referrals, and Related SEC MUIs, Investigations, Actions, and Outcomes, Fiscal Years 2003-2006

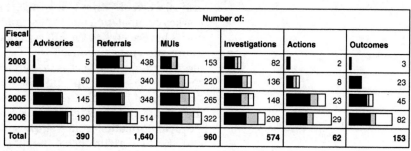

Fiscal year	Number of:					
	Advisories	Referrals	MUIs	Investigations	Actions	Outcomes
2003	5	438	153	82	2	3
2004	50	340	220	136	8	23
2005	145	348	265	148	23	45
2006	190	514	322	208	29	82
Total	390	1,640	960	574	62	153

☐ Other

▨ Market manipulation

■ Insider trading

Source: GAO.

Limited Search Capabilities of the SRO System and Lack of Linkage to Case Tracking System May Limit Management of Process and Staff Analysis

SEC's SRO system featured limited capability to electronically search information on advisories and referrals and may limit Enforcement staff's ability to efficiently monitor unusual market activity, make subsequent decisions about opening MUIs and investigations, and manage the SRO advisory and referral process. As we have previously discussed, federal internal control standards state that management needs relevant, reliable, and timely communications relating to internal and external events. In addition, these standards state that the information should be distributed in a form and time frame that permits management and others who need it to perform their duties efficiently.

SEC developed the SRO system to receive and store advisory and referral information from SROs and enable SEC staff to make initial decisions about which SRO-identified market activities to investigate. The system primarily receives information on unusual market activity based on SRO surveillance of trades among stock issuers. This information includes the name of the security issuer; the date of the unusual activity; and a description of the type of activity, among other data. The SRO system also stores narrative attachments, which the SROs provide to SEC, that contain additional information about individuals or entities, such as investment advisers or hedge funds, associated with unusual market activity. While the system allows OMS staff to search by issuer, the narrative information cannot be easily searched in the system; instead, the attachments must be individually opened and read. An Enforcement branch chief noted that narrative information can help establish patterns of behavior that are critical when SEC tries to investigate potentially fraudulent activity, such as market manipulation and insider trading. Furthermore, only OMS branch chiefs have access to the SRO system, so attorneys who need that information have to consult with OMS branch chiefs or contact SRO staff directly, rather than access that information electronically. In addition, since the referral receipt and case tracking systems are not linked, management is unable to readily assess the efficiency and effectiveness of the referral and investigation processes. For example, SEC is unable to extract information from a single source on how long it takes both SROs and SEC to work through different stages of cases over time, from referral receipt (SRO system) to opening MUIs and conducting investigations (case tracking system).[30] SEC headquarters and regional office officials noted that receiving information in a timely manner is critical to the investigative steps of assembling the facts of the case and collecting evidence on those potentially involved with unusual market activity. To obtain this information and customized reports and statistics on Enforcement operations, division officials said they must submit requests to SEC's OIT and then wait for OIT staff to respond to the request. As noted in our 2007 report on Enforcement Division operations, these requests may take several days to 1 week to complete. Having recognized system limitations, SEC officials have undertaken efforts to make improvements to CATS by developing a new case information management system called the Hub. However, these planned improvements do not address limitations of the SRO system and do not include expanded linkages between the SRO system and CATS.[31]

Conclusions

SEC's oversight of SRO enforcement programs has produced positive outcomes. For example, in response to an OCIE recommendation, SROs in the options market have developed a new surveillance authority, which is

---

[30]Calculating certain durations included in this report required us to manually merge data from the SRO and case tracking systems.

[31]GAO, *Securities and Exchange Commission: Additional Actions Needed to Ensure Planned Improvements Address Limitations in Enforcement Division Operations*, GAO-07-830 (Washington, D.C.: Aug. 15, 2007) for more information on CATS management and reporting limitations and SEC's ongoing efforts to create the Hub to improve Enforcement information system capabilities.

GAO-08-33 Securities and Exchange Commission

intended to improve coordination among SROs in monitoring the markets for insider trading and investigating any resulting alerts. The equities markets are expected to soon follow with a similar plan. SEC, through its Enforcement Division, has worked with SROs to detect and respond to potential securities laws violations. Between fiscal years 2003 and 2006, SEC responded to an increasing number of SRO referrals—a large percentage of which are related to insider trading—with an increasing number of investigations and enforcement actions. SEC has started to incorporate the results of SRO internal audits into its on-site inspections, which helps to leverage resources. In addition, the agency plans to expand its oversight of SRO functions to include reviews of the internal audit function—with an emphasis on independence, staffing levels, and scope of coverage. Such reviews could help ensure that SROs are effectively assessing risks, instituting appropriate controls, and carrying out their responsibilities.

However, several opportunities exist to enhance the efforts used by SEC to oversee SROs and, particularly, their enforcement programs. Specifically, OCIE examiners are conducting inspections of SRO enforcement programs without formal guidance. Although our review of a sample of inspections found that examiners have developed a methodology for reviewing SRO enforcement programs, the lack of written guidance—which establishes minimum standards and quality controls—could limit OCIE's ability to provide reasonable assurances that its inspection processes and products are subject to basic quality controls in such areas as examination planning, data collection, and report review. Moreover, the lack of formal guidance could result in individual inspection teams creating data collection and other examination tools that otherwise would be centralized and more efficiently shared across inspection teams.

Furthermore, OCIE's recent internal guidance on the use of SRO internal audit-related reports does not address the use of these reports for risk-assessment and inspection planning purposes, as we have previously recommended. We continue to believe that the use of these reports when conducting risk assessments and determining the scope of an upcoming inspection could allow OCIE to better leverage its inspection resources, especially if OCIE determines that the reports produced by SRO internal audit functions are reliable. As OCIE officials noted, they plan to begin assessing SRO internal audit functions in 2008, including the quality and reliability of their work products, although they have not yet developed guidance for inspection staff on conducting these reviews. By not considering the work and work products of the SRO internal audit function in its inspection planning process, OCIE may be duplicating SRO efforts and not maximizing the use of its limited resources. OCIE also may be missing an opportunity to better monitor the effectiveness of the SRO regulatory programs (including enforcement programs) between inspections.

SEC also has an opportunity to leverage the work of SRO internal audit functions in its assessment of information security at SROs. Since ARP Policy Statements specifically are intended to oversee systems essential to market operations, Market Regulation officials do not target enforcement-related databases for specific review. Although SROs have assessed the security controls of these databases, Market Regulation officials have little knowledge of the content or comprehensiveness of these audits. As a result, Market Regulation cannot determine whether SROs have taken the appropriate steps to ensure the security of this sensitive information. Market Regulation could facilitate this evaluation by making certain that enforcement-related databases continue to be periodically reviewed by SROs, and that these reviews are comprehensive and complete.

Both OCIE and Enforcement could benefit from improvements to information technology systems when overseeing SROs. OCIE currently lacks a system that tracks the status of inspection recommendations. OCIE officials told us that a new examination tracking database is in development that will allow OCIE to track the implementation of inspection recommendations as well as software that will allow OCIE to generate management reports from this database. By ensuring these system capabilities, OCIE management could improve its ability to monitor the implementation of OCIE recommendations, and begin developing measures for assessing the effectiveness of its program.

Finally, while SEC has responded to a significant increase in SRO referrals between fiscal years 2003 and 2006, Enforcement's systems for receiving referrals and tracking the resulting investigations have limited capabilities for searching and analyzing information related to these referrals. Enforcement is currently working to address some limitations in its case tracking system; however, this effort does not include making improvements to the separate system used to receive and manage SRO referrals. By including system improvements to allow electronic access to all of the information contained in advisories and referrals submitted by SROs, generate management reports, and provide links to the case tracking system, Enforcement could enhance its ability to efficiently and effectively manage SRO advisories and referrals and conduct analyses that could contribute to improved SEC planning, operations, and oversight.

Recommendations for Executive Action

To enhance SEC oversight of SROs, we recommend that the SEC Chairman take the following three actions:

- establish a written framework for conducting inspections of SRO enforcement programs to help ensure a reliable and consistent source of information on SRO inspection processes, minimum standards, and quality controls; and, as part of this framework, broaden current guidance to SRO inspection staff on the use of SRO internal audit reports to direct examiners to consider the extent to which they will rely on reports and reviews of internal and external audit and other risk-management systems when planning SRO inspections;

- ensure that Market Regulation makes certain that SROs include in their periodic risk assessment of their IT systems a review of the security of their enforcement-related databases, and that Market Regulation reviews the comprehensiveness and completeness of the related SRO-sponsored audits of their enforcement-related databases; and

- as part of the agency's ongoing efforts to improve information technology capabilities,

    - ensure that any software developed for tracking SRO inspections includes the ability to track and report SRO responses to and implementation status of OCIE inspections recommendations and

    - consider system improvements that would allow Enforcement staff to electronically access and search all information in advisories and referrals submitted by SROs and generate reports that would facilitate monitoring and analysis of trend information and case activities.

Agency Comments and Our Evaluation

We requested comments on a draft of this report from SEC. SEC provided written comments on the draft, which we have reprinted in appendix V. SEC also provided technical comments on a draft of the report, which were incorporated in this report as appropriate. In its written comments, SEC agreed with our recommendations. SEC noted that OCIE will provide SRO inspectors with written guidance on its risk-scoping techniques and compiled summary of inspection practices. In addition, OCIE plans to assess the quality and reliability of SRO internal audit programs and determine whether, and the degree to which, inspections can be risk-focused on the basis of SRO internal audit work. SEC also noted that it is developing a database to track the status of SRO inspection recommendations and provide management reports and that this enhancement should create additional efficiencies for inspection planning purposes. SEC's Market Regulation will implement our recommendation to ensure that enforcement-related databases continue to be periodically reviewed by SRO internal audit programs, and that these reviews are comprehensive and complete. Furthermore, Enforcement plans to consider recommended system improvements to more effectively manage the advisory and referral processes.

As agreed with your office, unless you publicly announce its contents earlier, we plan no further distribution of this report until 30 days after its date. At that time, we will send copies of this report to interested congressional committees and the Chairman of the Senate Committee on Finance. We will also send a copy to the Chairman of the Securities and Exchange Commission. We will also make copies available to others upon request. The report will be available at no charge on the GAO Web site at http://www.gao.gov.

If you or your staff have any questions regarding this report, please contact me at (202) 512-8678 or hillmanr@gao.gov. Contact points for our Offices of Congressional Relations and Public Affairs may be found on the last page of this report. Key contributors to this report are listed in appendix VI.

Sincerely yours,

Richard J. Hillman,
Managing Director, Financial Markets
    and Community Investment

Scope and Methodology

To discuss the overall structure of the Securities and Exchange Commission's (SEC) inspection program—more specifically, its approach to inspections of self-regulatory organizations' (SRO) surveillance, investigative, and enforcement programs (enforcement programs)—we reviewed and analyzed documentation of all 11 inspections that SEC's Office of Compliance Inspections and Examinations (OCIE) completed from March 2002 through January 2007 of enforcement programs related to the former NASD and the New York Stock Exchange (NYSE). We also reviewed and analyzed an OCIE memorandum to the Commission describing the SRO inspection process, staffing data provided by OCIE, and our prior work. Furthermore, we observed a demonstration of various information technology systems that NASD used to monitor the markets and track investigations and disciplinary actions. Finally, we reviewed and summarized the enforcement actions brought by SEC against SROs from 1995 to 2007. We also conducted interviews with staff from OCIE, NASD, and NYSE.

To evaluate certain aspects of SEC's inspection program, including guidance and planning, the use of SRO internal audit products, and the tracking of inspection recommendations, we reviewed OCIE inspection guidance related to the review of NASD district offices and SRO internal audit reports, guidance for bank examiners from the Board of Governors of the Federal Reserve System and the Office of the Comptroller of the Currency, inspection guidelines developed by the inspectors general, and our prior work. In addition, we reviewed SEC guidance for conducting reviews of SRO information technology (IT) related to market trading operations and regulatory fee remittance, and NASD and NYSE internal and external audits of IT security. Furthermore, we reviewed internal control standards for the federal government and conducted interviews with officials from OCIE and SEC's Division of Enforcement (Enforcement) on their respective procedures for ensuring that SROs implement inspection recommendations and remedial actions required as part of enforcement actions. We also conducted interviews with staff from OCIE, SEC's Division of Market Regulation and Office of Information Technology, NASD, and NYSE.

To describe the SRO referral process and recent trends in referral numbers and related SEC investigations, and evaluate SEC's information system for advisories and referrals, we observed a demonstration from Enforcement staff on the capabilities of their IT systems, analyzed data from SEC's SRO Referral Receipt System (SRO system) and Case Activity Tracking System (CATS), and interviewed Enforcement, NASD, and NYSE staff to determine how SEC manages the processes for receiving SRO referrals and conducting subsequent investigations. In particular, to understand trends in SRO advisories, referrals, and subsequent SEC investigations, we requested and analyzed data from SEC's referral and case tracking systems from fiscal years 2003 through 2006. We analyzed the data to provide descriptive information on the number of SEC's advisories, referrals, matters under inquiry (MUI), investigations, actions, and case outcomes during the period. We also analyzed these data by manually merging records from the SRO system and CATS to obtain descriptive data on the amount of time it takes SROs to identify unusual market activity and convey that information to SEC, as well as how long it takes SEC to respond by opening MUIs and investigations and achieving case outcomes. We inquired about checks SEC performs on the data and deemed the data reliable for the purposes of addressing our objectives. When calculating the average duration of stages to process SRO referrals, we distinguished between case stages that featured both open and close dates and those that were open or active as of the date we received data from SEC, and we reported duration information accordingly. In addition, to calculate case stage durations, we consulted with SEC and SRO staff to distinguish between initial and updated referrals and performed duration calculations using initial referrals only to avoid double counting that could skew the average duration results.

We performed our work in Washington, D.C.; New York, New York; and Rockville, Maryland, between September 2006 and September 2007 in accordance with generally accepted government auditing standards.

SEC Oversight of SRO Enforcement Programs Related to Insider Trading

SRO surveillance, investigative, and disciplinary programs are designed to enforce SRO rules and federal securities laws related to insider trading—the buying or selling of a security by someone who has access to material, nonpublic information about the security—and are subject to SEC oversight through periodic inspections by OCIE. In January 2007, OCIE completed a sweep inspection (a probe of specific activities across all or a sample of SROs) of SRO enforcement programs related to insider trading. As a result of OCIE's inspection, the options SROs submitted a plan to SEC to create a more uniform and coordinated method for surveillance and investigation of insider trading in the options markets, and the equities SROs indicated their intent to submit a similar plan. From fiscal years 2003 through 2006, SEC significantly increased the number of investigations that related to insider trading.

SROs Coordinate with SEC and Use Surveillance, Investigative, and Disciplinary Programs to Enforce Insider Trading Rules and Laws

SROs employ enforcement programs to enforce SRO rules and federal securities laws related to insider trading. Insider trading is illegal because any trading that is based on this information is unfair to investors who do not have access to the information. When persons buy or sell securities on the basis of information not generally available to the public, investor confidence in market fairness can be eroded. Information that could be exploited for personal gain by insiders include such things as advance knowledge of mergers or acquisitions, development of a new drug or product, or earnings announcements. While company insiders (e.g., directors and senior executives) may be the most likely individuals to possess material, nonpublic information, others outside of the company also may gain access to the information and use it for their personal gain. For example, employees at a copy store who discovered material, nonpublic information while making presentation booklets for a firm could commit insider trading if they traded on that information prior to it being made public.

To detect insider trading, SROs have established electronic surveillance systems that monitor their markets for aberrational movements in a stock's price or volume of shares traded, among other things, and generate alerts if a stock's price or volume of shares traded moves outside of set parameters. These systems link trade activity data to news and research about corporate transactions (such as mergers, acquisitions, or earnings announcements); public databases of listed company officers and directors; and other internal and external sources of information to detect possible insider trading. For example, the NASD Securities Observation News Analysis and Regulation system combines trade activity on NASDAQ, the American Stock Exchange, and the over-the-counter markets with news stories and other external sources of information to detect potential instances of insider trading and other potential violations of federal securities laws or NASD rules.[1]

SRO staff review the thousands of alerts generated by the electronic surveillance systems annually to identify those that are most likely to involve insider trading or fraud and warrant further investigation. In conducting reviews of these alerts, SRO staff consider such factors as the materiality of news, the existence of any previous news announcements, and the profit potential. If, in reviewing the trading associated with the alert, SRO staff determines there is a strong likelihood of insider trading, they can expand this review to a full investigation. In the course of a full investigation, SROs gather information from their member broker-dealers and the issuer of the traded stock to determine whether there is any relationship between those individuals who traded the stock and those individuals who had advance knowledge of the transaction or event. For example, SRO staff will typically request from their member broker-dealers the names of individuals and organizations that traded in advance of a corporate transaction or event, a process known as bluesheeting.[2] These data are then cross-referenced with information the SRO staff obtain from the issuer of the stock, including a chronology of the events leading up to the corporate transaction or event and the names of individuals who had knowledge of inside information.

SROs have created technology-based tools to assist in the identification of potential repeat offenders. For example, SROs can compare their blue sheets to a database called the Unusual Activity File (UAF), which includes data on suspicious trading activity identified by all SROs that are part of the

---

[1]In July 2007, SEC approved the establishment of the Financial Industry Regulatory Authority (FINRA). FINRA consolidated the former NASD (which provided regulatory services to markets such as the American Stock Exchange and NASDAQ) and the member regulation, enforcement, and arbitration operations of NYSE Regulation. NYSE Regulation, however, continues to be responsible for monitoring trading activity on the NYSE market and conducting investigations of suspicious trades. Because this consolidation occurred after our audit work was complete, we chose to refer to the former NASD, and not FINRA, throughout this report.

[2]When bluesheeting a broker-dealer, SROs request detailed information about trades performed by the firm and its client, including the stock's name, the date traded, price, transaction size, and a list of the parties involved. The questionnaires SROs use came to be known as blue sheets because they were originally printed on blue paper. Today, due to the high volumes of trades, this information is provided electronically.

Intermarket Surveillance Group, to help identify persons or entities that have been flagged in prior referrals or cases related to insider trading, fraud, or market manipulation.[3] Some SROs have also developed other databases for their internal use. For example, NASD developed a database similar to the UAF for suspicious trading activity it has identified. NYSE also has developed a database of individuals who are affiliated with entities that it considers at high risk for insider trading.

When SROs find evidence of insider trading involving their members, they can conduct disciplinary hearings and impose penalties ranging from disciplinary letters to fines to expulsion from trading and SRO membership. Because SROs do not have jurisdiction over entities and individuals that are not part of their membership, they refer suspicious trading on the part of nonmembers directly to Enforcement. Although Enforcement staff do not have direct access to SRO surveillance data or recidivist databases like the UAF, several staff told us they are able to obtain any needed information from the SRO analysts who made the referrals.

Data we reviewed from NASD and NYSE between fiscal years 2003 and 2006 showed that the SROs referred significantly more nonmembers to SEC for suspected insider trading than they referred members internally to their own Enforcement staff. According to SRO staff, this may be because the majority of the entities and individuals who trade on the basis of material, nonpublic information do so as a result of connections to the issuers of the stocks traded, rather than the investment advisor role that would involve member firms and their employees. Another possible explanation, according to SRO staff, is that the individual registered persons (SRO members) typically conceal their misconduct by trading in nominee accounts or secretly sharing in the profits generated by nonregistered persons involved in the scheme. As a result, they said that concealed member misconduct is often exposed through evidence developed by SEC using its broader jurisdictional tools after the SRO has referred a nonmember to SEC. For example, they said that SEC can expose the concealed member misconduct by fully investigating the nonregistered person's activities through documents such as telephone and bank records

---

[3]The purpose of the ISG is to provide a framework for the sharing of information and the coordination of regulatory efforts among exchanges trading securities and related products to address potential intermarket manipulations and trading abuses.

obtained by subpoena. SEC also has the ability to issue subpoenas to nonmembers to appear for investigative testimony.

SEC's Inspection Program to Oversee SRO Enforcement Efforts Has Identified Opportunities for SROs to Improve Surveillance of Insider Trading

OCIE assesses the effectiveness of SRO regulatory programs, including enforcement programs, through periodic inspections. OCIE officials said that when evaluating SRO enforcement programs related to insider trading, their objective is to assess whether the parameters of the surveillance systems are appropriately set to detect abnormal movements in a stocks' price or volume and generate an alert, the extent to which SRO policies and procedures direct the SRO staff to conduct thorough reviews of alerts and resulting investigations, and the extent to which SRO analysts comply with these policies and procedures and apply them consistently. OCIE staff said that when reviewing case files, one of their priorities is to assess the evidence upon which the SRO analyst relied when deciding to terminate the review of an alert or investigation. For example, they said that they will assess whether the analyst selected an appropriate period to review trading records (because suspicious trades may have occurred several days or weeks prior to the material news announcement), whether the analyst reviewed the UAF and internal databases for evidence of recidivism, and whether the analyst appropriately reviewed any other stocks or entities related to the trading alert.

OCIE officials said that in light of the recent increase in merger and acquisition activity and the increased potential for insider trading, SROs are making greater efforts to detect attempts of individuals or firms to benefit on both sides of a merger or acquisition.[4] For example, they said that where previously it was common for one SRO analyst to investigate any alerts generated from the movement of the target firm and for a different analyst to investigate any alerts generated from the movement of the acquiring firm—making it difficult to identify an account or individual that may have traded on both sides of the acquisition—SRO policies now generally require one analyst to review and investigate both stocks involved in a merger or acquisition. Generally speaking, mergers and

---

[4]Referrals from SROs grew from 438 to 514, or an increase of 17 percent, between fiscal years 2003 and 2006. The numbers of SEC investigations and enforcement actions also showed a corresponding increase. We found that almost 91 percent of all advisories and almost 80 percent of SRO referrals sent to SEC during this period involved suspected insider trading activity, which Enforcement and SRO staff attributed to increased merger and acquisition activity.

acquisitions present opportunities for insider trading because the acquiring company generally must pay more per share than the current price, causing the target firm's stock price to increase. In this case, an individual with knowledge of an upcoming acquisition could purchase the target's stock prior to the announcement and then sell for a gain the stock after the announcement at the higher price. An individual also could sell any holdings or sell short the stock of the acquiring firm if the individual believed that the acquiring firm's stock price would decrease after the announcement.[5] Finally, an individual could attempt to buy the target firm and sell (or short sell) the acquiring firm in an attempt to benefit on both sides of an acquisition.

In January 2007, OCIE completed sweep inspections of surveillance and investigatory programs related to insider trading at 10 SROs. As a result of its inspections, OCIE identified opportunities for improved coordination and standardization among SROs in monitoring and investigating possible insider trading. OCIE found that because each SRO at the time maintained its own surveillance systems, the variances in the system parameters could result in the possibility that stock or option movements might generate an alert at one SRO but not another. Furthermore, OCIE found that because each SRO was responsible for monitoring every stock that traded on its market, the SROs were duplicating the initial screening of alerts.

As a result of OCIE's then ongoing inspection, the options SROs submitted a plan to SEC to create a more uniform and coordinated method for the regulation, surveillance, investigation, and detection of insider trading in the options markets. SEC approved the plan, called Options Regulatory Surveillance Authority (ORSA), in June 2006.[6] The plan allows the options SROs to delegate part or all of the responsibility of conducting insider trading surveillance and investigations for all options trades to one or more SROs, with individual SROs remaining responsible for the regulation of their respective markets and retaining responsibility to bring disciplinary proceedings as appropriate. ORSA has currently delegated this surveillance

---

[5]A short sale is the sale of a borrowed security, commodity, or currency with the expectation that the asset will fall in value. For example, an investor who borrows shares of stock from a broker and sells them on the open market is said to have a short position in the stock. The investor must eventually return the borrowed stock by buying it back from the open market. If the stock falls in price, the investor buys it for less than he or she sold it, thus making a profit.

[6]*Order Approving Options Regulatory Surveillance Authority Plan*, Exchange Act Release No. 34-53940 (June 5, 2006), published in 71 Fed. Reg. 34399 (2006) (Order).

and investigative responsibility to the Chicago Board Options Exchange. The ORSA plan also provides for the establishment of a policy committee that is responsible for overseeing the operation of the plan and for making all relevant policy decisions, including reviewing and approving surveillance standards and other parameters to be used by the SRO performing the surveillance and investigative functions under the plan. The committee also will establish guidelines for generating, reviewing, and closing insider trading alerts; specific and detailed instructions on how analysts should review alerts; and instructions on closing procedures, including proper documentation and rationale for closing an alert. OCIE officials stated that they have met regularly with the options SROs to monitor the implementation of the plan and the development of related policies and procedures. According to the Commission, the ORSA plan should allow the options exchanges to more efficiently implement surveillance programs for the detection of insider trading, while eliminating redundant effort. As a result, OCIE officials believe the plan will promote more effective regulation and surveillance.

According to OCIE officials, the equities SROs are currently drafting a similar plan for coordinating insider trading surveillance in equities markets. However, instead of designating one SRO to conduct all insider trading-related surveillance, OCIE officials said that the current draft proposal would require each listing market, or its designee, to conduct insider trading surveillance for its listed issues, regardless of where trading in the security occurred. This includes reviewing alerts, pursuing investigations, and resolving cases through referrals (to SEC) or disciplinary action. OCIE officials said that the equities SROs anticipate voting on a proposed plan at the October 2007 Intermarket Surveillance Group meeting and to submit the plan to SEC by the end of 2007.

SEC Civil Enforcement Actions against SROs, January 1995–September 2007

Pursuant to sections 19 and 21 of the Securities Exchange Act of 1934, SEC may bring enforcement actions against an SRO either in federal court or through an administrative proceeding if it has found that an SRO has violated or is unable to comply with the provisions of the act and related rules and regulations, or if it has failed to enforce member compliance with SRO rules without reasonable justification or excuse. The act authorizes SEC to seek a variety of sanctions in an administrative proceeding, including the revocation of SRO registration, issuance a cease-and-desist order, or censure. An SRO may also agree to undertake other remedial actions in a settlement agreement with SEC. In addition to the remedies available in administrative enforcement action, a district court in a civil enforcement action may impose civil monetary penalties and has discretion to fashion such other equitable remedy it deems appropriate under the circumstances.

Tables 2 through 11 summarize the 10 civil enforcement actions SEC brought against SROs from January 1995 through September 2007. For this report, we have included only those findings and terms of settlement related to SRO surveillance, investigative, or disciplinary programs (enforcement programs). As such, these summaries do not necessarily identify all findings and terms of the settlement agreements.

Table 2: Summary of Findings, Enforcement Actions, and Outcomes Brought under the SEC Administrative Proceeding of August 8, 1996

Type of action	Order Instituting Public Administrative Proceedings Pursuant to Section 19(h)(1) of the Securities Exchange Act of 1934, Making Findings and Imposing Remedial Sanctions Administrative Proceeding File No. 3-9056
Respondent	National Association of Securities Dealers (NASD)
Action date	August 8, 1996
Key findings	SEC made the following findings: • NASD failed to conduct an appropriate inquiry into an anticompetitive pricing convention among NASDAQ market makers; • NASDAQ market makers followed and enforced a pricing convention used to determine the increments in which they would adjust their displayed quotes; • market makers shared proprietary information about customer orders, collaborated and coordinated their activities, failed to honor quotations, and failed to timely report trades; and • market-making firms held excessive amounts of influence in NASD oversight, its committees, and the disciplinary process.
Outcomes	Without admitting or denying SEC's findings, NASD agreed to take the following actions: • take significant steps to restructure its governance and regulatory structure, including ensuring a substantial independent review staff reporting directly to NASDAQ's Board of Governors; • increase staff positions for Enforcement, Examination, and Market Regulation; • institute the participation of professional hearing officers to preside over disciplinary proceedings; • institute measures to enhance the enforcement of the trade reporting, firm quote, customer limit order handling, and other market-making rules; • develop an enhanced audit trail system; and • enhance its systems for trading and market surveillance.

Source: SEC.

Table 3: Summary of Findings, Enforcement Actions, and Outcomes Brought under the SEC Administrative Proceeding of June 29, 1999

Type of action	Order Instituting Public Administrative Proceedings Pursuant to Section 19(h)(1) of the Securities Exchange Act of 1934, Making Findings and Ordering Compliance with Undertakings Administrative Proceeding File No. 3-9925
Respondent	New York Stock Exchange, Inc. (NYSE)
Action date	June 29, 1999
Key findings	SEC made the following findings: NYSE • failed to enforce compliance with Section 11(a) of the Exchange Act; Rule 11a-1; and NYSE Rules 90, 95, and 111, which are aimed at preventing independent floor brokers (IFB) from exploiting their position for personal gain; • failed to take appropriate action to police the manners in which IFBs were compensated; • failed to establish surveillance procedures designed to evaluate how commissions were computed; and • suspended its routine IFB surveillance for extensive periods.
Outcomes	Without admitting or denying SEC's findings, prior to settlement with SEC, NYSE took certain steps that included: • providing new or additional guidance regarding IFB compensation arrangements; • designing and implementing a program to require the examination of all IFBs within 2-year cycles; • amending NYSE rules to require certain members to make and keep written records of compensation arrangements; • adopting new rules requiring all members to disclose their own account or accounts over which they exercise any discretion; • maintaining error accounts to facilitate NYSE monitoring for trading abuses; and beginning to develop a floor audit trail for the electronic capture of certain order information. NYSE also agreed to further take the following actions: • enhance and improve its regulation of IFBs, member firm floor brokers, specialists, registered competitive market makers, and competitive traders; • file an affidavit with the Commission setting forth the details of NYSE's compliance with the undertakings described; • retain an independent consultant for review of NYSE's rules, practices, and procedures applicable to floor members and recommend changes to these rules as necessary; and • maintain a substantial independent internal review staff with adequate resources to regularly review all aspects of NYSE.

Source: SEC.

Table 4: Summary of Findings, Enforcement Actions, and Outcomes Brought under the SEC Administrative Proceeding of September 11, 2000

Type of action	Order Instituting Public Administrative Proceedings Pursuant to Section 19(h)(1) of the Securities Exchange Act of 1934, Making Findings and Imposing Remedial Sanctions Administrative Proceeding File No. 3-10282
Respondents	American Stock Exchange (AMEX), Chicago Board Options Exchange (CBOE), Pacific Exchange (PCX), and Philadelphia Stock Exchange (PHLX)
Action date	September 11, 2000
Key findings	SEC made the following findings: • The options exchanges significantly impaired the operations of the options market by following a course of conduct under which they refrained from joint listing a large number of options. • The exchanges inadequately surveilled their markets for potential rules violations, failed to conduct thorough investigations, and failed to adequately enforce rules applicable to members on their floors. • The exchanges failed to enforce compliance with rules that promote competition, enhance investor protections, and prohibit anticompetitive conduct. • The exchanges generally lacked automated surveillance systems, and relied too heavily on complaints. • In many cases, the exchanges did not take appropriate enforcement actions when violations were uncovered. • In cases where enforcement actions were taken, the exchanges did not impose sanctions adequate to provide reasonable deterrence against future violations.
Outcomes	Without admitting or denying SEC's findings, The SROs agreed to take the following actions: • eliminate advance notice to any other market of the intention to list an existing option or new option; • eliminate any provisions to the Joint Plan that would prevent a market from commencing to list or trade any option listed on another market or an option that another market has expressed and intent to list; • enhance and improve its surveillance, investigative, and enforcement processes and activities with a view toward preventing and eliminating harassment, intimidation, refusals to deal, and retaliation against market participants acting competitively; • acting jointly, design and implement a consolidated options audit trail system; and • enhance and improve its surveillance, investigative, and enforcement processes and activities for options order handling rules, limit order displays, priority rules, trade reporting, and firm quote rules.

Source: SEC.

Table 5: Summary of Findings, Enforcement Actions, and Outcomes Brought under the SEC Administrative Proceeding of September 30, 2003

Type of action	Order Instituting Public Administrative Proceedings Pursuant to Sections 19(h) and 21C of the Securities Exchange Act of 1934, Making Findings, and Imposing a Censure, a Cease-and-Desist Order and Other Relief Administrative Proceeding File No. 3-11282
Respondent	Chicago Stock Exchange (CHX)
Action date	September 30, 2003
Key findings	SEC made the following findings: CHX • failed to implement surveillance systems and procedures to detect and prevent violations of its firm quote, trading ahead, and limit order display rules; • relied on an ineffective manual review process; • did not provide staff with adequate and consistent standards and guidelines to assist them; • failed to take adequate disciplinary action against members when violations were detected; and • failed to take adequate disciplinary action against recidivists or violators of multiple rules.
Outcomes	Without admitting or denying SEC's findings, CHX agreed to take the following actions: • increase its staffing for enforcement programs and implement new protocols and guidelines regarding surveillance; • begin offering training sessions regarding compliance with trading rules; • enhance its exception reports and computer logic; • create a regulatory oversight committee; and • hire an outside consultant to conduct a comprehensive review of CHX's trading floor surveillance and enforcement programs as well as report on its findings.

Source: SEC.

Table 6: Summary of Findings, Enforcement Actions, and Outcomes Brought under the SEC Administrative Proceeding of February 9, 2005

Type of action	Report of Investigation Pursuant to Section 21(a) of the Securities Exchange Act of 1934 Regarding the Nasdaq Stock Market, Inc., as Overseen by Its Parent, the National Association of Securities Dealers
Respondent	National Association of Securities Dealers (NASD)
Report release date	February 9, 2005
Key findings	SEC made the following findings: • NASD and NASDAQ did not adequately address a large number of wash trades and matched orders in March 2002 by MarketXT, an ECN, NASD member, and registered broker-dealer, which were reported through NASDAQ. • NASDAQ failed to communicate to NASD Regulation the observations of NASDAQ staff members relating to the trading described above. • NASDAQ supervisors failed to take any steps to ensure that the suspicious trades were referred to NASD Regulation. • NASD Regulation's automated surveillance programs did not independently detect the suspicious conduct.
Outcomes	Remedial steps taken by NASDAQ: • created a NASDAQ Regulation Group; • had the NASDAQ Office of General Counsel (OGC) formalize the procedure for responding to information that suggests a possible rule violation; • instituted mandatory companywide employee education on regulatory responsibilities; • amended its code of conduct to require that employees refer potential regulatory violations to OGC or other appropriate NASDAQ department; and • refunded the consolidated tape for the fees it received associated with MarketXT trading. Remedial steps taken by NASD: • formed a committee of the NASD board to review a number of governance issues, and studied the standards for NASD review of NASDAQ board items; • retained a law firm to review the interactions between NASD and NASDAQ in the regulatory area; and • NASD board appointed a special committee with the charge of reviewing the relationship between NASD and NASDAQ, and NASD's oversight of that relationship.

Source: SEC.

Table 7: Summary of Findings, Enforcement Actions, and Outcomes Brought under the SEC Administrative Proceeding of April 12, 2005

Type of action	Order Instituting Public Administrative Proceedings Pursuant to Sections 19(h)(1) and 21C of the Securities Exchange Act of 1934, Making Findings, Ordering Compliance with Undertakings, and Imposing a Censure and a Cease-and-Desist Order Administrative Proceeding File No. 3-11892
Respondent	New York Stock Exchange, Inc. (NYSE)
Action date	April 12, 2005
Key findings	SEC made the following findings: NYSE • failed to properly detect, investigate, and discipline widespread unlawful proprietary trading by specialists on the floor of the exchange; • surveillance systems failed to detect the vast majority of improper trades due to NYSE's reliance on automated systems whose parameters and procedures were unnecessarily and unreasonably broad; • Office of Market Surveillance policies improperly limited the cases selected for further examination; • inadequate referral procedures and investigation policies further limited the cases examined; and • additional and repeat violations were often treated with additional informal actions, rather than being escalated to formal disciplinary actions.
Outcomes	Without admitting or denying SEC's findings, NYSE agreed to take the following actions: • commit to biannual, third-party audits of its regulatory function, of which SEC receives a copy, and • establish a pilot program for sufficient audio and video equipment to capture floor trading activity occurring at a specialist's post.

Source: SEC.

Table 8: Summary of Findings, Enforcement Actions, and Outcomes Brought under the SEC Administrative Proceeding of May 19, 2005

Type of action	Order Instituting Administrative and Cease-and-Desist Proceedings Pursuant to Sections 19(h) and 21C of the Securities Exchange Act of 1934, Making Findings, and Imposing Sanctions Administrative Proceeding File No. 3-11931
Respondents	National Stock Exchange (NSX) and the CEO of NSX
Action date	May 19, 2005
Key findings	SEC made the following findings: NSX • failed to enforce compliance by its dealer firms with the market order exposure rule and the customer priority (trading ahead) rule; • did not update its interpretation after decimalization and did not bring to SEC's attention its intention to enforce the rule according to its old interpretation; • did not conduct surveillance until 2004 for violations of its customer priority rule, which prohibited designated dealers from trading ahead of customer orders in their possession; • failed to develop and implement an automated surveillance report to detect trading ahead; • when trading-ahead violations were identified, failed to perform a follow-up review of that member's trading to determine whether additional violations had occurred; and • failed to preserve e-mails made or received in the course of its business or self-regulatory activity for a minimum of 5 years.
Outcomes	Without admitting or denying SEC's findings, NSX agreed to take the following actions: • create a regulatory oversight committee (ROC); • adopt structural protections to ensure the NSX's regulatory functions shall be independent from the commercial interests of NSX and its members; • adopt internal procedures that provide for the ROC and NSX Board to approve the issuance of regulatory circulars; • create and maintain complete and detailed minutes of all NSX board meetings; • implement and maintain automated daily surveillance for potential violations of the NSX and Exchange Act rules; • require NSX designated dealers to implement system enhancements; • design and implement a mandatory training program for NSX's regulatory department that addresses compliance with the federal securities laws and NSX rules; and • hire an independent consultant to conduct a comprehensive review of NSX's policies and procedures for rulemaking, surveillance, and examination programs.

Source: SEC.

Table 9: Summary of Findings, Enforcement Actions, and Outcomes Brought under the SEC Administrative Proceeding of June 1, 2006

Type of action	Order Instituting Administrative and Cease-and-Desist Proceedings, Making Findings, and Imposing Remedial Sanctions and a Cease-and-Desist Order Pursuant to Sections 19(h) and 21C of the Securities Exchange Act of 1934 Administrative Proceeding File No. 3-12315
Respondent	Philadelphia Stock Exchange (PHLX)
Action date	June 1, 2006
Key findings	SEC made the following findings: PHLX • did not adequately surveil for violations of rules relating to priority of options orders; • failed to properly surveil for firm quote rule violations; • did not implement any type of surveillance of its equities market to monitor its specialists for compliance with the firm quote rule; • generated exception reports using improper parameters, which excluded certain transactions that were potentially priority rule or firm quote violations; • generated an excessive number of alerts and false positives in exception reports for front-running violations, making the reports ineffective; and • did not maintain adequate written surveillance procedures for PHLX investigators reviewing the surveillance reports.
Outcomes	Without admitting or denying SEC's findings, PHLX agreed to take the following actions: • obtain outside counsel and consultants to conduct a complete review of its regulatory programs, augment the ranks of regulatory staff and management, and significantly increase its regulatory budget in an effort to enhance its regulatory program and • implement a mandatory, annual training program for all floor members and members of PHLX regulatory staff responsible for surveillance, investigation, examination, and discipline of floor members that addresses compliance with the federal securities laws and PHLX rules.

Source: SEC.

Table 10: Summary of Findings, Enforcement Actions, and Outcomes Brought under the SEC Administrative Proceeding of March 22, 2007

Type of action	Order Instituting Administrative and Cease-and-Desist Proceedings, Making Findings, and Imposing Remedial Sanctions, a Censure, and a Cease-and-Desist Order Pursuant to Sections 19(h)(1) and 21C of the Securities Exchange Act of 1934 Administrative Proceeding File No. 3-12594
Respondent	American Stock Exchange (AMEX)
Action date	March 22, 2007
Key findings	SEC made the following findings: • From 1999 through June 2004, AMEX had critical deficiencies in its surveillance, investigative, and enforcement programs for ensuring compliance with its rules as well as federal securities laws. • AMEX's continual regulatory deficiencies during this period resulted in large part from its failure to pay adequate attention to regulation, put in place an oversight structure, or dedicate sufficient resources to ensure that the exchange was meeting its regulatory obligations. • AMEX failed to surveil for, or take appropriate action relating to, evidence of violations of firm quote, customer priority, limit order display, and trade reporting rules. • Under a 2000 enforcement action, the Commission ordered AMEX to enhance and improve its regulatory programs for surveillance, investigation, and enforcement of the options order handling rules. AMEX also was required to provide Commission staff with annual affirmations detailing its progress in complying with the 2000 order. AMEX failed to comply with these obligations. • AMEX employed incorrect or deficient parameters in some of its surveillance systems.
Outcomes	Without admitting or denying SEC's findings, AMEX agreed to take the following actions: • file with the Commission a proposed rule change to identify and implement enhancements to its trading systems for equities and options reasonably designed to prevent specialists from violating AMEX's priority rules; • enhance its training program and implement mandatory annual training for all floor members; • commencing in 2007, and for each of the successive 2-year periods (6 years), retain a third-party auditor to conduct a comprehensive audit of AMEX's surveillance, examination, investigative, and disciplinary programs relating to trading applicable to all floor members; and • submit an auditor's report to its board of governors and the directors of OCIE and Market Regulation, and include the audit report in its annual report. SEC ordered that AMEX shall • develop a plan of corrective action, including dates for implementation, which they are to keep and provide to the Commission upon request.

Source: SEC.

Table 11: Summary of Findings, Enforcement Actions, and Outcomes Brought under the SEC Administrative Proceeding of September 5, 2007

Type of action	Order Instituting Administrative and Cease-and-Desist Proceedings, Making Findings, and Imposing Remedial Sanctions and a Cease-and-Desist Order Pursuant to Sections 19(h) and 21C of the Securities Exchange Act of 1934 Administrative Proceeding File No. 3-12744
Respondent	Boston Stock Exchange, Inc. (BSE) and the former President of BSE
Action date	September 5, 2007
Key findings	SEC made the following findings: • BSE failed, between 1999 and 2004, to enforce certain of its rules intended to prevent BSE broker-dealer specialist firms from trading in a way that benefited them, while disadvantaging their customers who were trying to buy and sell stock. • BSE failed to develop and implement adequate procedures for surveillance of violations of its customer priority rules. • BSE's failure to implement programming changes and to otherwise conduct effective surveillance allowed hundreds, if not thousands, of violations per day to go undetected. • Violations continued even after the Commission staff had repeatedly warned BSE of the need to improve surveillance systems. • BSE internal documents demonstrated awareness of BSE's surveillance system's flaws at all levels of the organization, and these flaws resulted in the system yielding too many exceptions to be useful in detecting priority rule violations.
Outcomes	Without admitting or denying SEC's findings, prior to settlement with SEC, BSE took certain steps that included • replacement of senior management responsible for regulatory compliance during the period in which the violations discussed herein occurred. BSE also agreed to take the following actions: • Within 90 days after the issuance of the Order, enhance its existing training programs for all members of the regulatory staff responsible for surveillance, investigation, examination, and discipline. • Retain a third-party auditor, not unacceptable to the Commission, to conduct a comprehensive audit of BSE's surveillance, examination, investigation, and disciplinary programs. • The auditor must submit an audit opinion to BSE's Board of Governors, and the following Commission officials: Director of OCIE, Director of Division of Market Regulation, and Director of the Boston Regional Office. • BSE must implement the auditor's recommendations. BSE may disagree with the recommendations and may attempt to reach an agreement with the auditor. If such agreement cannot be reached, the auditor's recommendations will be binding.

Source: SEC.

Analyses of SEC-Provided Data on Various Case Stages

Tables 12 to 22 include analyses of data from fiscal years 2003 to 2006 provided by SEC from its SRO system and CATS. This appendix provides specific analyses on the number and types of advisories; referrals; matters under inquiry (MUI); investigations; case actions; and case outcomes, by fiscal year and SRO. It also describes reasons that SEC closed MUIs and provides data on average and median investigation durations, by type of investigation.

Table 12: Number and Type of Advisories, Fiscal Years 2003-2006

Fiscal year	Number of insider trading advisories	Number of market manipulation advisories	Number of all other types of advisories	Total advisories
2003	5	0	0	5
2004	48	1	1	50
2005	135	3	7	145
2006	166	7	17	190
Total	**354**	**11**	**25**	**390**

Source: GAO.

Table 13: Number of Advisories, by Fiscal Year and SRO, Fiscal Years 2003-2006

Fiscal year	Number of advisories from NASD[a]	Number of advisories from NYSE	Number of advisories from all other SROs	Total advisories
2003	0	0	5	5
2004	0	1	49	50
2005	0	16	129	145
2006	5	18	167	190
Total	**5**	**35**	**350**	**390**

Source: GAO.

[a]NASD officials noted that they develop information on unusual market activity as well as they possibly can and typically submit referrals, rather than advisories.

Table 14: Number and Type of Referrals, Fiscal Years 2003-2006

Fiscal year	Number of insider trading referrals	Number of market manipulation referrals	Number of all other types of referrals	Total referrals
2003	283	53	102	438
2004	321	10	9	340
2005	306	24	18	348
2006	386	41	87	514
Total	1,296[a]	128	216	1,640

Source: GAO.

[a]Our analysis shows that from fiscal years 2003 to 2006, almost 80 percent of SRO referrals involved potential insider trading activity, and that almost 60 percent of investigations opened by SEC involved potential insider trading. A SEC branch chief noted that the differences in percentages reflect the difficulty of proving insider trading cases.

Table 15: Number of Referrals, by SRO and Fiscal Year, Fiscal Years 2003-2006

Fiscal year	Number of referrals from NASD	Number of referrals from NYSE	Number of referrals from all other SROs	Total referrals
2003	247	70	121	438
2004	177	39	124	340
2005	130	89	129	348
2006	201	142	171	514
Total	755	340	545	1,640

Source: GAO.

Table 16: Number and Type of Matters Under Inquiry, Fiscal Years 2003-2006

Fiscal year	Number of insider trading MUIs	Number of market manipulation MUIs	Number of all other types of MUIs	Total MUIs
2003	86	40	26	152
2004	147	44	29	220
2005	154	74	37	265
2006	172	89	61	322
Total	559	247	154	960

Source: GAO.

Table 17: Numbers of Matters Under Inquiry Closed and Associated Reasons for
Closure, Fiscal Years 2003-2006

Reason for closure	Number of MUIs closed	Percentage of total MUIs closed
Closed into investigation	605	63.0%
Evidence not appropriate for investigation	253	26.4
Closed due to resource limits	38	4.0
Case transferred to another SEC office	29	3.0
Merged with another case	20	2.1
Inappropriate for SRO action	12	1.3
Sent to state or local agency	1	0.1
Sent to SRO for further action	1	0.1
Sent to another federal agency	1	0.1
Total	960	100

Source: GAO.

Table 18: Number and Type of Investigations Resulting from SRO Referrals, Fiscal
Years 2003-2006

Fiscal year	Number of insider trading investigations	Number of market manipulation investigations	Number of all other types of investigations	Total investigations
2003	50	17	15	82
2004	89	26	21	136
2005	84	38	26	148
2006	111	60	37	208
Total	334	141	99	574

Source: GAO.

Table 19: Average and Median Investigation Duration, by Type of Investigation, Fiscal Years 2003-2006

Type of investigation	Average duration, by days
All investigations	534
Insider trading	554
Market manipulation	543
All investigations, except insider trading	495

Source: GAO.

Table 20: Number, Type, and Duration of Investigations, Fiscal Years 2003-2006

Fiscal year	Open investigations (as of 4/18/07)		Closed investigations	
	Number	Days of average duration	Number	Days of average duration
2003	36	1,426	46	741
2004	68	1,114	68	565
2005	98	744	50	434
2005	183	372	25	260
Total/Average	385	697	189	534

Source: GAO.

Table 21: Number and Type of Case Actions, Fiscal Years 2003-2006

Fiscal year	Number of insider trading actions	Number of market manipulation actions	Number of all other types of actions	Total actions
2003	2	0	0	2
2004	4	2	2	8
2005	15	5	3	23
2006	13	4	12	29
Total	34	11	17	62

Source: GAO.

Table 22: Number and Type of Case Outcomes, Fiscal Years 2003-2006

Fiscal year	Number of insider trading outcomes	Number of market manipulation outcomes	Number of all other types of outcomes	Total outcomes
2003	3	0	0	3
2004	20	1	2	23
2005	33	4	8	45
2006	40	10	32	82
Total	96	15	42	153

Source: GAO.

Comments from the Securities and Exchange Commission

CHRISTOPHER COX
CHAIRMAN
————
HEADQUARTERS
100 F STREET, NE
WASHINGTON, DC 20549

REGIONAL OFFICES
ATLANTA, BOSTON, CHICAGO,
DENVER, FORT WORTH,
LOS ANGELES, MIAMI, NEW YORK,
PHILADELPHIA, SALT LAKE CITY,
SAN FRANCISCO

UNITED STATES
SECURITIES AND EXCHANGE COMMISSION

November 2, 2007

Mr. Richard Hillman
Managing Director
Financial Markets and Community Investment
U.S. Government Accountability Office
441 G Street, N.W.
Washington, DC 20548

Dear Mr. Hillman:

Thank you for the opportunity to review and comment on the draft GAO report on the SEC's oversight of self-regulatory organizations. The SEC staff is separately providing you with technical comments on the draft report.

As you know, SROs play a critical role in monitoring and regulating activities in the securities industry. The SEC, in turn, operates a robust program for oversight of the SROs' operations. The GAO reviewed the structure and evaluated certain components of the SEC's inspection program for SROs, as well as the SEC's process for receiving, and following up on, referrals from the SROs of possible securities laws violations.

SRO Inspections Program. SRO inspections conducted by the SEC's Office of Compliance Inspections and Examinations (OCIE) play a particularly critical part in the oversight of SROs. As noted in the report, to help ensure that SROs are fulfilling their regulatory responsibilities, OCIE conducts both routine and special inspections of SRO regulatory programs. The report notes that routine inspections assess SRO enforcement, arbitration, listings, and member examination programs at regular intervals. Special inspections are conducted as warranted and encompass follow-up work on prior recommendations or enforcement actions, investigations of tips or reports, and sweep inspections. The report summarizes these inspection processes and also makes several recommendations for possible enhancement to existing processes.

Specifically, GAO recommends that inspection staff establish a written framework for conducting inspections of SRO enforcement programs and that, as part of that framework, inspection staff broaden the current examination guidance to direct that examiners consider the extent to which they will rely on the reports of reviews conducted by SROs' internal audit and other risk-management programs. GAO also recommends that the software program under development for tracking SRO inspections include the ability to track the status of the SROs' implementation of corrective actions.

CHAIRMANOFFICE@SEC.GOV
WWW.SEC.GOV

Mr. Richard Hillman
Page 2

As reflected in the report, OCIE believes that the considerable differences among SRO
regulatory programs make it difficult to adopt a uniform manual for conducting inspections of
SRO enforcement programs. To date, such inspections have been specifically tailored and risk-
focused on the particular operations of the SRO inspected. For example, in determining the
scope and nature of each inspection, examiners are directed to, among other things, review
previous inspection reports of the SRO to be inspected (including the SRO's response to the
report and all follow-up communications between the SRO and OCIE) and conduct appropriate
pre-inspection research about the nature of the SRO's regulatory program. Nonetheless, we
agree that a manual could help ensure quality standards and controls. Consistent with GAO's
recommendation, OCIE will prepare written guidance for SRO inspectors regarding the
inspection of SRO enforcement programs, including risk-scoping techniques, and a compiled
summary of inspection practices. We believe that this guidance may be particularly useful in
training new examiners.

As noted in the report, OCIE also plans to assess the quality and reliability of the SROs'
internal audit programs and to determine whether, and the extent to which, inspections can be
risk-focused based on the SRO's own internal audit work. As GAO learned during the review,
internal audit programs vary among the SROs, so the determination of whether the SEC can
effectively rely on SRO internal audit work product must be based on careful analysis.

Finally, as the report notes, OCIE is developing a tracking database for SRO inspections
that will, among other things, track the implementation of SRO inspection recommendations and
generate reports. This enhancement should create additional efficiencies when inspectors are
planning and conducting future inspections of SROs and is consistent with your
recommendation.

Oversight of Security of SRO Databases. GAO also reviewed the process used by the
Division of Market Regulation to conduct regular security reviews of the SROs' information
technology systems, in accordance with SEC guidance. As noted in the report, these reviews are
intended to oversee SRO systems that are essential to market operations. GAO's report states
that NASD (now FINRA) and NYSE have conducted internal and external reviews that
concluded that both have adequate controls in place to protect sensitive enforcement-related data.
GAO recommends that the Division of Market Regulation make certain that enforcement-related
databases continue to be periodically reviewed by SROs' internal audit programs and that these
reviews be comprehensive and complete. The staff of the Division of Market Regulation will
implement this recommendation.

SRO Referrals and Advisories. GAO also reviewed the process by which SROs refer
matters to the SEC's Division of Enforcement, recent trends in the number of referrals and
related SEC enforcement investigations, and the information system maintained by the Division
of Enforcement for these advisories and referrals. As noted in the report, the number of
advisories and referrals from SROs have increased in recent years, and there has been a
corresponding increase in the number of Commission enforcement investigations and
enforcement actions based on SRO referrals. Most of these referrals involved potential insider
trading that was detected through SROs' surveillance systems.

Mr. Richard Hillman
Page 3

As the report notes, the Division of Enforcement is currently implementing a new case
tracking system. To enhance the ability of the Enforcement staff to manage the advisory/referral
process and to efficiently access information from those referrals and advisories, the report
recommends that the Enforcement staff consider system improvements that would allow the staff
to electronically access and search all information in referrals and advisories submitted by SROs
and generate reports. The report suggests linking the referral and advisory system to the case
tracking system in order to provide Enforcement staff with electronic access to referral and
advisory information, and the report recommends that the staff be able to generate reports. We
agree that additional information technology changes such as these may help the Enforcement
staff to effectively analyze trends, manage current caseloads, and focus areas of investigation.
We will assess the feasibility of the recommended system improvements.

*   *   *

We appreciate GAO's attention to these issues and as detailed above will address the
report's recommendations.

Sincerely,

Christopher Cox
Chairman

GAO Contact and Staff Acknowledgments

GAO Contact

Richard J. Hillman, (202) 512-8678, hillmanr@gao.gov

Staff Acknowledgments

In addition to the contact named above, Karen Tremba (Assistant Director), Nina Horowitz, Stefanie Jonkman, Matthew Keeler, Marc Molino, Omyra Ramsingh, Barbara Roesmann, and Steve Ruszczyk made key contributions to this report.

GAO's Mission	The Government Accountability Office, the audit, evaluation, and investigative arm of Congress, exists to support Congress in meeting its constitutional responsibilities and to help improve the performance and accountability of the federal government for the American people. GAO examines the use of public funds; evaluates federal programs and policies; and provides analyses, recommendations, and other assistance to help Congress make informed oversight, policy, and funding decisions. GAO's commitment to good government is reflected in its core values of accountability, integrity, and reliability.
Obtaining Copies of GAO Reports and Testimony	The fastest and easiest way to obtain copies of GAO documents at no cost is through GAO's Web site (www.gao.gov). Each weekday, GAO posts newly released reports, testimony, and correspondence on its Web site. To have GAO e-mail you a list of newly posted products every afternoon, go to www.gao.gov and select "E-mail Updates."
Order by Mail or Phone	The first copy of each printed report is free. Additional copies are $2 each. A check or money order should be made out to the Superintendent of Documents. GAO also accepts VISA and Mastercard. Orders for 100 or more copies mailed to a single address are discounted 25 percent. Orders should be sent to: U.S. Government Accountability Office 441 G Street NW, Room LM Washington, DC 20548 To order by Phone: Voice: (202) 512-6000 TDD: (202) 512-2537 Fax: (202) 512-6061
To Report Fraud, Waste, and Abuse in Federal Programs	Contact: Web site: www.gao.gov/fraudnet/fraudnet.htm E-mail: fraudnet@gao.gov Automated answering system: (800) 424-5454 or (202) 512-7470
Congressional Relations	Gloria Jarmon, Managing Director, jarmong@gao.gov, (202) 512-4400 U.S. Government Accountability Office, 441 G Street NW, Room 7125 Washington, DC 20548
Public Affairs	Chuck Young, Managing Director, youngc1@gao.gov, (202) 512-4800 U.S. Government Accountability Office, 441 G Street NW, Room 7149 Washington, DC 20548

Lightning Source UK Ltd.
Milton Keynes UK
UKOW02f2237100314

227915UK00006B/37/P